THE GENESIS OF GENDER

ABIGAIL FAVALE

The Genesis of Gender

A Christian Theory

IGNATIUS PRESS   SAN FRANCISCO

Cover art:
Harald Slott-Møller, *Adam and Eve*, 1891 (detail)
National Gallery of Denmark, Copenhagen
Public domain

Cover design by John Herreid

© 2022 by Ignatius Press, San Francisco
All rights reserved
ISBN 978-1-62164-408-8 (PB)
ISBN 978-1-64229-217-6 (eBook)
Library of Congress Control Number 2021940718
Printed in the United States of America ∞

For our sons and daughters.
May they know their true worth.

CONTENTS

ACKNOWLEDGMENTS

This has been a difficult book to bring forth, and I have many skilled midwives to thank.

First, my gal pals: Hayley McCullough, Cassie Meadows, Jessica Rolfe, Merissa Zielinksi, and Erika Barber. Your prayers and encouragement buoyed me up through many moments of fear and self-doubt.

To my soul-friend Lindsay Tsohantaridis especially, who read through the rough cut, and whose friendship is one of my great consolations.

To all who have shared their stories, speaking honestly about gender dysphoria and transition, especially Daisy Chadra, Laura Reynolds, and Adelynn Campbell, who entrusted their stories to me, a sacred thing. And to one particular woman, who prefers anonymity, who showed me how best to support the dignity of intersex people like herself.

To those who helped me think through my own thoughts, saying yes to a stranger asking for a Zoom chat: Angela Franks, Erika Bachiochi, Stephen Adubato, Isaiah Jones, and Benjamin Boyce.

To Artur Rosman, editor of *Church Life Journal*, who graciously gave me permission to pillage some words from my *Church Life* essays and weave them into this book.

To Corynne Staresinic, founder of *The Catholic Woman*, who helped me envision what Catholic feminism could look like.

To Mark Brumley, for taking a chance on me, and to Suzanne Lewis, Thomas Jacobi, and Abigail Tardiff, all good shepherds throughout the editing process.

To Michael and our children, who, more than anything, reveal to me daily the depth of divine love and the sacramental beauty of the body.

Abigail Favale
October 15, 2021
Feast of Saint Teresa of Ávila

Heretic

In the spring of 2015, I was teaching a course on gender theory at a Christian university. This was a course I'd taught for years, but never in quite the same way. Gender theory was ever morphing, as were my students, and I was pivoting constantly, trying to keep up with the latest jargon and trends. This time was different. I was in the midst of two dramatic upheavals in my personal life: the birth of my second child, which happened in the middle of the semester, and a tumultuous conversion to Catholicism, which was upending everything I thought I knew. I found myself both giving birth and being born—my body turned inside out to bring forth a daughter; my soul turned inside out to make room for Christ. Each of these births, like every birth, was an engulfing paradox of beauty and agony.

My physical labors tend to go quickly. Spiritual labor, not so much. I began that semester as a half-brewed convert: technically Catholic, but not yet inwardly Catholic. I was in a strange and dizzying in-between. When I joined the Church in 2014, I assumed I would become a "cafeteria Catholic", lugging my cherished progressive beliefs into the Church and taking shelter under the canopy of conscience. Then something terrible happened. My conscience started to rebel. The progressive beliefs I was carrying began to feel less like personal belongings and more like baggage: burdensome and out of place.

The world I'd inhabited comfortably as a feminist academic started to make less sense. I was like Plato's unhappy cave dweller, stumbling out of the murk into blinding daylight for the first time. The shadows on the stone walls behind me, once so clear and disturbingly real, now seemed cartoonish and oversized. Yet moving beyond the cave was terrifying; my eyes had not adjusted to a world lit up by the sun, so I lingered in the entrance for a while, stranded in the half-light.

Teaching gender theory in that state was bewildering, to put it mildly. While discussing essays I'd taught a dozen times, I was suddenly plagued by unbidden questions, noticing gaps and inconsistencies that had never troubled me before. Over the semester, it became increasingly clear to me—in little epiphanies of horror—that I'd been living in a cave for over a decade, mistaking it for reality. In pursuing my love for women's literature and my abiding interest in women's experiences, I had entered a field of study that came prepackaged with its own totalizing worldview, a worldview I gradually absorbed. I'd become an ideologue without realizing it.

I remember one particular class session, when my students and I were wrangling with an essay by Judith Butler, a prominent gender theorist. In the essay, Butler rolls out her concept of gender performativity: gender as something we *do*, rather than something we *are*. (I'll discuss Butler in more detail in chapter 3.) Like most critical theorists, Butler writes in all but impenetrable prose; nonetheless, my students readily embraced her idea of gender as a performance. What they didn't fully recognize is that Butler asserts gender is *only* a performance, that "women" don't really exist, and that any truth claim is ultimately an exercise of power. These ideas, which might not have been so appealing to my students, remained well hidden below the surface, obscured under opaque jargon. My students skimmed along the topsoil, grasping a few blooms here and there, but they never got a good look at the root. Only now catching my first real glimpse, I wasn't much help to them.

I left class that day feeling defeated and unsure why. I'd taught this text to undergraduates before, many times, with an untroubled conscience. In fact, I'd often felt *good* about exposing my students to heady and trendy theories about gender. When they voiced newfound uncertainty and confusion, as they usually did at the end of the course, I'd feel satisfied, as if my central task as a gender studies professor was to disrupt and unsettle their tidy and simplistic views, to expose them to irresolvable complexity. Now that work of disorientation, without any effort at reorientation, began to unsettle me. My conscience, after giving me reassuring high-fives for the past decade, was now clearing her throat in the backroom of my mind and asking: So, is any of this *true*?

In this state of unease, I sought the advice of an older professor I respected. I rushed to his office straight from home, my hair still wet from a recent shower. I was newly back from maternity leave, always five minutes behind and sweating profusely, trying to cram all I could into the three-hour windows between breastfeeding sessions. I showed up with a Diet Coke in hand, thinking I would be having a nice, casual chat with a colleague. Within five minutes I was in full-blown confession mode, disclosing the indictments of my conscience not to a priest, but to a gray-bearded Quaker with a Gandalf vibe. "I feel like I've been giving my students poison to drink", I said. For so many years, I'd been careless, careless with their minds and, most disturbingly, their souls.

The professor listened quietly to me, as was his way. He tends to speak few words, but those words are usually wise and rarely what you want to hear. He could have coddled me, told me I'd done what I thought was right at the time, that I was being too hard on myself. Instead, he said, in an Appalachian drawl, "You know that verse in Matthew? The one that says if anyone causes the little ones to stumble, it would be better for him to have a millstone hung around his neck and be drowned in the sea? I've always thought it would be a good idea for us professors to have that tattooed on our arms."

That's what I was feeling: the damn millstone. In truth, it had been around my neck for years, but at least now I was feeling the weight of it. That much was a comfort.

I left his office with a little more clarity about what I *didn't* want to do. I didn't want to keep teaching gender theory as a set of value-neutral ideas, without giving any attention to the worldview operating in the background. I didn't want my endgame to be confusion. I understood what *not* to do, but was less sure about what *to* do.

If gender theory was, at root, an ideological discipline, had I simply wasted my education? Was there nothing good here, nothing salvageable? I did not know how to integrate these theories with my newfound Catholic identity—or whether I should even try. I had to keep climbing out of the cave, that much I knew, but was there nothing of value I could bring with me? I was experiencing a profound worldview dissonance, as if I'd been floating happily along on what I'd thought was a sturdy raft, only to discover I was straddling two separate logs that were drifting apart.

I suspect there are many women today who find themselves in a similar place: caught between worldviews, suspended between Christianity and the latest feminist trends, wondering how, if at all, those perspectives connect and overlap. Some feel this tension deeply, unsure how to reconcile the two. Others don't feel it at all, instead concluding that Christianity and feminism are so compatible they amount to roughly the same thing: to follow Jesus is to be a feminist. Then there are those who adopt feminism so wholeheartedly it becomes a religion, and any lingering Christian commitments gradually become vestigial or disappear altogether.

In my strange and meandering journey of faith, I've been all of those women.

Evangelical Feminist

I started college in the fall of 2001. The planes hit the Twin Towers two weeks into my first semester. The world was in turmoil, but all that was miles away; I was safely on the West Coast, preoccupied with the upheaval in my own small world. Leaving home felt like a prison break. I was eager to pursue the college promise of self-discovery—and to find a boyfriend as quickly as possible. At the time, I held typical Evangelical views about women; I toed the party line on things like male headship and female submission, at least if asked. Encouraged as I'd been from a young age to dream about my future husband, I kept a list of desired traits in the back of my journal. At the top of the list? "A leader in the home and in the world". Ever a creature of contraries, I also kept a list of all the boys I'd kissed, a number that ramped up into double digits the summer before college.

Despite my obligatory nod toward male authority, I didn't have a good track record of embodying the submissive feminine ideal. I often found myself in male-dominated spaces, like the boys' soccer team in high school and the philosophy classroom in college, and I'd manage to hold my own. I was ambitious and competitive, feisty when needed. I didn't fit the feminine mold (too much body hair, for one thing) and my awareness of this fact heightened during that first year of college. Debates about women's roles, which had seemed far off to me as a teenager, now gained urgency. Marriage, family life, career: these were no longer just future fantasies but looming prospects. The question of my identity and purpose as a woman became pressing.

I entered college assuming, as I'd been taught, that feminism was a harmful ideology at odds with Christianity. Not that anyone in my Evangelical church or small Mormon hometown ever really mentioned feminism. The most I heard was Rush Limbaugh occasionally railing against "Feminazis" on the car radio. I thought of feminists as shrill, liberal women with short hair and pantsuits. It didn't take long for this caricature to fall by the wayside. Within nine short months of entering college, I was writing a term paper entitled "God Is a Feminist" and emailing it to my no-doubt scandalized parents.

What sparked this sudden shift? Reading the Bible. As a cradle Evangelical I'd done plenty of Bible reading, but only in typical piecemeal fashion: a memory verse here, a chapter or passage there. In college, however, I was required to read a whole biblical book in one stretch, and I discovered some strange, murky corners in the Bible I thought I knew. I was caught off guard by verses about women covering their heads and keeping silent during church, or even more perplexing: women as the image and glory of man, and men as the image and glory of God.[1] That one sent me spinning. Are men closer to God than women are? Despite growing up in a nesting doll of religious conservatism—an Evangelical bubble inside a Mormon bubble—I had never been so directly confronted

---

[1] 1 Corinthians 11:7.

with what seemed to be a hierarchy of value between women and men, and from the Word of God, no less.

I instinctively recoiled from the idea that women have less value in the eyes of God. But I wanted to be able to reconcile my belief in men and women's equal dignity with the authoritative words of Scripture. My professor didn't have a satisfactory interpretation, and neither did my classmates. Feeling lost, I took myself to the library, searching for answers. Wandering those aisles, I made a discovery that would reorient the trajectory of my intellectual life: feminist biblical interpretation.

This discovery sparked what you might call my own "first wave" as a feminist: Evangelical feminism. For the next two years or so, I focused my energy on interpreting Scripture in a way that affirmed an egalitarian perspective on men and women. I found a golden hermeneutical key in a snippet from Galatians 3:28—"there is neither male nor female; for you are all one in Christ Jesus." I used that key to unlock the puzzling verses that had troubled me. Meanwhile, my broader religious views remained more or less Evangelical. I still relied on Scripture as the ultimate authority, with the caveat that it must be interpreted correctly; I had faith in Christian revelation and Christ's salvific work. I saw no tension between feminism and Christianity, as I understood them, and I busied myself with the work of convincing others of their compatibility.

My "second wave" of feminism began when I was a junior. There was a new professor on campus who was a vocal feminist, and I took her class on women in the Bible. When we got to those pesky Pauline passages in the New Testament, I sat back and waited to be taught what I already knew: Paul is not sexist; we just have to read him correctly.

To my surprise, the professor pivoted to make another argument entirely: Paul is indeed sexist, but we can just ignore those bits of Scripture, because they were corrupted by the patriarchal culture of the time. My first reaction to this was frustration; I knew my classmates, who were skeptical about feminism, would retreat from any perspective that played fast and loose with the Bible, and I'd been hoping to win some feminist converts.

Despite my initial vexation, the class gradually began to reshape my view of Scripture. By the end of the term, I had wholeheartedly adopted the professor's way of thinking and reading. The Bible was no longer the Word of God, something trustworthy and deeply true; I saw it as a man-made artifact and an instrument of women's oppression. For the first time, I began to feel a tension, even a chasm, between Christianity and feminism. I was decidedly on the feminist side, glaring suspiciously across at Scripture and tradition.

The following semester, I went to Oxford to study medieval women writers. I spent four months immersed in the works of Hildegard of Bingen, Julian of Norwich, and Christine de Pizan—all deeply Christian writers and faithful daughters of the Church. Strangely, I did not see these women as representative of tradition; I saw them as rogue players, whose voices had been suppressed. I found a handy little sourcebook of anti-woman material in the writings of various Church Fathers that I took as representative of Christian tradition as a whole. Without reading any of the primary sources in their entirety, I contented myself with these excerpts, plucked from their full context, to blacklist Augustine, Ambrose, John Chrysostom, *et al.* and support my presumption that Christian tradition is anti-woman.

I quickly acquired a reductive and bifurcated understanding of Church history. I saw the women writers I had newly discovered as marginalized figures, even though

Hildegard wielded enormous influence in her day and has since been declared a saint and doctor of the Church. My grasp of "tradition" was hopelessly impoverished, but I was unaware of this. I had been raised in a corner of Christianity that was more or less ahistorical, one that viewed our local church as a seamless extension of the earliest Christians in the New Testament. The intervening centuries, the gradual working out of creeds, canon, and doctrine—all of this was skipped over entirely. I was not even self-consciously Protestant, unaware that Evangelicalism is itself a tradition, the newest kid on a longstanding block. I knew the Bible well, but I was unaware of its interpretative heritage. I naively assumed that my familiarity with Scripture made me an expert on Christianity writ large, and I wasted no time in hastily constructing a flimsy scarecrow version of it, one I could easily tear down.

Looking back, I can see clearly that both of my first feminist phases were characterized by enthusiastic cherry-picking. As an egalitarian feminist, I selected the verses that appeared to affirm that perspective, like Galatians 3:28, and used those verses to reinterpret the ones that seemed at odds with egalitarianism. As a critical feminist, I homed in on the passages that were flagrantly sexist and used those to confirm my conclusion that the Bible, and thus Christianity as a whole, was fundamentally patriarchal and in dire need of feminist reform. Instead of wading into the tension created by these apparent conflicts within Scripture, I made a classic move: resolving the tension by doing away with it altogether.

I caught a glimpse of a third way in Oxford—one that avoided the well-worn paths of misogynist hierarchy on the one hand and egalitarian sameness on the other. I wrote my term paper that semester on Hildegard's cosmology, focusing specifically on her understanding of man and woman in the created order. Differences between men and women have too often been used to justify a strict hierarchy of value and roles between the sexes. In the effort to reject this, feminist thought has typically regarded sexual difference itself with hostility and has downplayed difference in order to affirm equal dignity. Hildegard's mystical theology, conveyed through rich images rather than abstract propositions, conveys an understanding of difference that is harmonious and balanced, rather than hierarchical. I was able to recognize that her vision of complementarity was unlike the complementarity I'd been taught in Evangelical circles, and I also perceived that she was out of step with modern feminism, which is suspicious of the very concept of complementarity.

Somehow, Hildegard managed to balance equal dignity with meaningful difference, in a way I'd not yet encountered. I wish I'd followed that thread; perhaps it would have pulled me into the Christian cosmos earlier. Instead, I let it go and lost myself in the labyrinth of postmodern feminism for the next ten years.

Revisionist Feminist

This was the beginning of a new wave for me: revisionist feminism. I graduated from college and went to graduate school in Scotland to study women's writing and gender theory. By then, I was increasingly interested in French poststructuralist feminism. I was drawn to philosophers like Hélène Cixous and Luce Irigaray, who were doing strange and unsettling things with language. Reading their works was like entering a dream world, ducking just under the surface of conscious thought into a realm where words, images, and metaphors swirled around in dizzying eddies, creating pictures that moved and shimmered and dissolved. As an undergraduate philosophy major, I had grown tired of the desiccated language of analytic philosophy that seemed hopelessly removed from embodied experience. These French feminists were in the continental stream of philosophy, and the body, especially the bodies of women, loomed large in their writing. While Anglo-American feminists seemed to be doing their best to dodge the difference and specificity of the female body—its ability to gestate, to lactate, to give birth—the French feminists reveled in it. Cixous' work articulates a distinctly feminine mode of writing, drawing on the metaphorical richness of femaleness. "I write with white ink", she declares, as if she's sitting in her Parisian studio and dipping her fountain pen in breastmilk.

A month before I started my master's program in gender studies, I did something unconventional, at least for someone starting a master's program in gender studies. I got married. To a man, no less. At the age of twenty-two. This was so perplexing to my feminist comrades that they nicknamed me "the queer wife"; in the world of feminist academia, I was an oddity, already settled into a heterosexual marriage while most of my fellow students were freewheeling through ever-shifting lesbian love triangles.

I was odd in another way: I was religious. Or, I wasn't *not* religious. To an actual religious person, I would have seemed quite secular. The entire time I lived in Scotland, I did not enter a church, aside from roaming the ruins of the old cathedral on the edge of the North Sea. This cathedral, built in the twelfth century, was once the largest church in Scotland and a vibrant hub of Catholic Christianity, serving as the seat of the Archdiocese of Saint Andrews. In 1559, the cathedral was ransacked by followers of John

Knox, the Protestant reformer, and within two years it was completely abandoned and left to ruin.

I had come to see Christianity as something like this derelict cathedral, a sacred structure that had been rightfully dismantled—not because of papist transgressions, but because of patriarchal ones. Instead of walking away from the ruins, I lingered among them, trying to rearrange the stones and rebuild. I wanted to remake the cathedral, as an act of revision rather than restoration. I wanted to construct a new Christianity, fully purged of sexism, hierarchy, and sin.

This work of religious revision became the focus of my doctoral dissertation, and the French feminists were my muses, especially the philosopher Luce Irigaray. Her work lent itself readily to this task of revision for two reasons: unlike many feminist philosophers, she places value on the religious dimension of human experience; and, as a thoroughgoing postmodernist, she places no limits on how freely and extensively one can revise.

Postmodernism, to put it simply, is a worldview that sees reality in terms of narratives that are created by human beings, rather than an order of objective truths that can be discovered by human beings. Postmodernism reflects a deep skepticism toward "metanarratives"—collective, explanatory narratives that give an overarching account of reality. Christianity, or any established religion, certainly counts as a metanarrative, as does an atheistic scientism. Postmodernism is equally skeptical of an Enlightenment understanding of reality as it is of a Christian one. Postmodernists don't necessarily reject the existence of God, but they do reject the knowability of God and objective truth. God is not a being who discloses himself to us through the created order and divine revelation; rather, "God" is merely a projection of human desires, a story we tell ourselves.

Irigaray's philosophy emphasizes the need for the concept of God as an ultimate limit or horizon toward which we can grow and develop as human beings. The problem, for Irigaray, is that this horizon has been defined by men, projected from male desire and experience. The task for women is to create a distinctively feminine understanding of God, one that can facilitate our "becoming" as women. Irigaray doesn't think that women need to be free from religion; rather, they need to belong to a religion of their own making.

During graduate school, I became a postmodern feminist in an Irigarayan mode. I envisioned reality as a closed dome overhead. I could look up at the dome and imagine that something mysterious and God-like was beyond it, but within the closed world under the dome, the only tool I had to access that "beyond" was language—words, metaphors, and images that, as human creations, would always fall short of capturing ultimate truth. The best I could do was play with those words and try to make them meaningful, knowing all the while that they would hit the impenetrable roof of the dome and bounce back.

There's something to this. Mystics, theologians, and doctors of the Church have always stressed that God is beyond finite human understanding and can never be fully understood. I was going a step farther, confusing "understandability" with "knowability". God is beyond our understanding, but *he is nonetheless knowable*, because he is able to make himself known. As a postmodernist, I focused all my attention on the inability of human language and understanding to reach out and fully grasp a divine being. I had lost sight of a divine being who reaches down to take hold of us.

Within this worldview, any claim to authoritative knowledge is simply an exercise of power. There is no authority, whether Scripture or a church magisterium, that has special access to truth, and so I could reject or accept any established doctrine at will. I saw Christianity as a narrative created by human beings and therefore open to revision by other human beings, like myself. In my dissertation, I analyzed novels written by women that challenged and modified traditional Christian narratives, and I saw this as a liberating task, a reclamation of power.

That was the full extent of my religious praxis during this period of my life. I did not pray. I did not attend a church. I did not read Scripture. I dissertated. I was a Christian only in the sense that the Christian narrative was the one I'd chosen to play with. From my postmodern vantage, that was enough.

There were moments, sometimes full days, of sudden lucidity. I would look up from a page I was writing or a text I was reading and think: *I'm just making stuff up.* In those moments, I had the fleeting, anxious sense that the work I was doing was not connected to any kind of genuine knowledge. Then the moment would pass; I'd shake off the sensation, dismissing it as grad student insecurity. Deep down, underneath the trendy postmodern jargon I'd internalized, my soul was still reflexively reaching for something true.

What disturbs me most about this period of my life is the cognitive dissonance I endured. I considered myself a Christian, yet I did not believe in anything resembling orthodoxy, and I had no active praxis whatsoever. I had left Christianity behind without recognizing it. My faith had been hollowed out from the inside, but because a thin outward shell remained intact, I did not face the reality that I was a Christian in name only. In belief, I was agnostic; in practice, an atheist.

One way of telling my story is to say that feminism led me away from Christianity. From a certain angle, this is true. Immersing myself in feminist philosophy, feminist biblical interpretation, and gender theory taught me to read the world—*especially* Christian Scripture and tradition—with a "hermeneutics of suspicion". I was trained to carry the assumption that sexism was always at play, in every text and every human interaction, and my job was to reveal it, to rip off the mask and yell, "Gotcha!" Every worldview rests on certain assumptions that are taken for granted, just as a house rests on a foundation. These principles are truth claims that are assumed rather than proved. Even postmodernism rests, albeit ironically, on the premise that no worldview premises are true. When I first encountered feminism, my foundation was a Christian one; I was approaching feminism from Christian premises. At some point, that flipped, and I was living on a different foundation, looking out the window at Christianity from afar. That shift is what caused my Christian faith to deteriorate, because the foundation of that faith had been displaced. My first principles, the premises on which my worldview rested, were now postmodernist, rather than Christian.

Heretical Feminist

There is, however, another side of this story to tell. There's the fact that my interest in feminism led me to study Hildegard of Bingen, the brilliant mystic who would become my confirmation saint ten years down the road. There's also the fact that Irigaray's philosophy played a part in my eventual turn toward the Catholic Church.

In the first year of my Ph.D. studies at Saint Andrews, when I was still floundering, trying to figure out what I was supposed to be doing, I was accepted into a doctoral seminar with Luce Irigaray, my philosopher hero. Banished as she was from French academia for being too much of an iconoclast—her first book, *Speculum of the Other Woman*, takes shots at established giants of the French intelligentsia, like Jacques Lacan—Irigaray did her teaching in the U.K., through annual week-long seminars that gathered doctoral students from all over the world to workshop their research with her. I was the youngest in the group and easily the most starstruck. I couldn't believe I was in the same room, around the same table, with my feminist hero. In between seminars, she would regale us with insider gossip about other French philosophers, like Hélène Cixous (who, according to Irigaray, is *absolutely terrifying*). I was so overcome with delirious elation and anxiety that I could barely eat, and I had to borrow melatonin from my jet-lagged American comrades in order to sleep.

When it came time to workshop my research, which was barely off the ground at that point, I explained that I was studying how contemporary women writers were reimagining traditional religious concepts and stories in their novels. Irigaray pushed back hard against my reliance on the concept of "imagination". She argued that it was too ethereal and conceptual, which played into an unhealthy dualism that prizes the realm of abstraction over the realm of embodiment. Rather than *imagination*, she urged, I should focus on *incarnation*.

This was a turning point. I recentered my dissertation on the idea of incarnation as a way out of dualism. "Incarnation" became the prominent theme of my intellectual life. I read and wrote and theorized about it for years; it became the fishing line that kept me tied to Christianity, because I recognized that the doctrine of the Incarnation sets Christianity apart from other religions.

Of course, there was an invisible irony at work—invisible to me then, but stark to me now. The "incarnation" I embraced was not a real incarnation but a conceptual one. I continued to duck the question of whether God *actually*, not just *metaphorically*, became man in Jesus Christ. But an incarnation that is only conceptual falls into the same trap of dualism I was trying to escape. To borrow a phrase from philosopher Charles Taylor, this was a purely "excarnate" incarnation, because what should be *embodied* is reduced to a theoretical idea.

Despite this irony, my preoccupation with incarnation was the golden hook that allowed divine grace to reel me into the Catholic Church. By the end of my twenties, I was spiritually starved. Toying with religious concepts and metaphors was not enough, precisely because they cannot be truly incarnational when cut off from the reality of *the* Incarnation, a reality that is made visible and tangible in the sacraments. I was tired of just thinking about incarnation; I needed to taste it, to taste *him*, the Word made flesh, and that eucharistic longing propelled me forward into a sudden and unexpected conversion.

I've written at length about this conversion elsewhere, in its full and bizarre complexity, but here I want to highlight just one key aspect.[2] It is a strange twist in my conversion story, strange at least for those who think there is nothing redeemable about feminist theory, that studying Irigaray is what set me on a winding road toward Catholicism. This dual truth, that feminist theory both led me away from and then back toward a deep Christian faith, is why I am not satisfied with simplistic accounts of feminism's influence, accounts that either demonize feminism

---

[2] See Abigail Favale, *Into the Deep: An Unlikely Catholic Conversion* (Eugene, OR: Cascade Books, 2018).

(sometimes quite literally) or overly glamorize it. Like most things in this world, especially most philosophies, there is in feminist thought a mixture of good and bad, truth and falsehood. It's overlooking that mix that can get one into trouble.

We need to take a hard look at feminism and distinguish the good from the bad. This is especially true now, because feminism, thanks to the internet and trickle-down academia, has gained widespread popularity. My experience as a Christian college student in the early 2000s is vastly different from the experience of my students now. I did not (at first) have any professors teaching about feminism in the classroom; it wasn't part of any designated reading list. I had to go out of my way to hunt down some dusty books in the library that had been tucked there since the 1980s, with few checkout stamps in the back cover. Most significantly, the internet was still in its lumbering toddler phase; "google" was not yet a verb, and social media did not exist. Considering these factors, it's a small miracle I became a feminist so quickly at an Evangelical college in 2001. I was an oddball. Over my four years, there were maybe a handful of other students I knew who would similarly identify as feminists. We were a vocal but small minority. I was quickly branded "that feminist girl" because there were so few vying for the title.

Now, twenty years later, my students inhabit a world where feminism has become mainstream, even in Christian circles. *Not* to be a feminist is a major *faux pas*, tantamount to being anti-woman. Pop feminist slogans, hashtags, and memes permeate social media, and the pressure to jump on the bandwagon is intense. Even in the Christian university where I teach, feminism has become part of the establishment. There are classes offered in gender theory and feminist philosophy, and concepts from feminist theory are part of the standard curriculum in certain disciplines like English literature and social work. I had to go out of my way to find feminism as a college student, but this is no longer necessary. Whether to identify as a feminist and to what degree are now unavoidable questions that young people have to confront.

This new reality became stark for me a couple of years ago, when one of my students came to confess something: she wasn't sure she was a feminist. She believed in equality between men and women, of course (and she herself was a talented, ambitious student who would be accepted into a top grad program), but she wasn't sure about the whole *package* of feminism. She couldn't comfortably admit this to her friend group, because nuanced positions weren't welcome. Either you identified as a feminist or you were a misogynist by default. When I was a student, the "sin" to confess was being a feminist. Now, it's transgressive *not* to be one.

There is ample room, and a great need, for an authentically Christian feminism. This is the "new feminism" John Paul II called for, a feminism that reclaims women's dignity and does not simply replicate masculine modes of domination.[3] I do have to warn you: being a Christian feminist means being a heretic, one way or another. You have to make a choice. Embracing Christian orthodoxy means rejecting certain feminist dogmas. Accepting those dogmas entails betraying some Christian beliefs. I've been a feminist heretic in both senses at different points in my life. Now, I'm doing my best to be a faithful daughter of the Church. If I am a feminist, I'm choosing to be a heretical one.

[3] John Paul II, encyclical letter *Evangelium vitae* (The Gospel of Life) (March 25, 1995), no. 99.

Two Paradigms

There is a danger in embracing feminism unthinkingly and letting it become a totalizing worldview, as I did. There is also a danger in dismissing feminism too hastily, because that leaves important concerns unaddressed. Despite feminism's conquest of the mainstream, girls and women are constantly bombarded with images that objectify and degrade them. Depression, anxiety, and self-harm are skyrocketing among preteen girls. That same demographic is, in exponential numbers, deciding to reject womanhood altogether and embrace a male identity. The questions that feminism seeks to address are still vital and relevant, even if the answers feminism provides are too often self-defeating.

We must engage the vital questions of personhood, sex, identity, and freedom at the level of worldview. This is why I was so distraught in 2015: I had come to realize that the gender theory I'd been teaching my students was often rooted in an underlying framework that is at odds with Christianity. I had not helped them see the incommensurability, because I'd been blind to it myself. I'd become an impassioned, oblivious Pied Piper.

While feminism has, at times, been a force of good in my life, it ultimately brought me to a place at odds with Christianity, a place I will call the *gender paradigm*. The gender paradigm affirms a radically constructivist view of reality, then reifies it as truth, demanding that others assent to its veracity and adopt its language.

According to the gender paradigm, there is no creator, and so we are free to create ourselves. The body is an object with no intrinsic meaning; we give it whatever meaning we want, using technology to undo what is perceived to be "natural". We do not *receive* meaning from God or our bodies or the world—we impose it. What we take to be "real" is merely a linguistic construct; ergo we should consciously wield language to conjure the reality we want. To be free is to transgress limits continually, to unfetter the will. "Woman" and "man" are language-based identities that can be inhabited by anyone. Because truth is just a story we tell ourselves, all self-told stories are true.

I'm adapting the word "paradigm" from philosopher Thomas Kuhn, who used this term to describe a model or framework for interpreting the world and the phenomena we experience. Kuhn invoked it to analyze the history of science. In this book, I'm analyzing the genealogy of gender, providing an account of how the gender paradigm emerged and how it compares to the paradigm of Catholic Christianity.

In the mid-twentieth century, a new way of categorizing men and women began to arise, one centered not on biological sex, but on *gender*. To understand how this paradigm developed, it is necessary to trace its roots in feminism. The feminist movement has given birth to many things: one of these is the popularization of gender, a concept that drives a wedge between sexed identity and embodiment. At first, this conceptual separation facilitated more complex discussions about cultural influences on sexed identity; in our time, however, the fissure has widened into a chasm. The word "woman" no longer belongs to female personhood at all.

I came to inhabit the gender paradigm through the gateway of feminist theory. My personal journey is something of an historical microcosm, because our culture entered the gender paradigm through the same door. Feminism and gender theory maintain strong familial ties. Aside from a dissident contingent of "gender critical" feminists, contemporary feminism has made a comfortable home for itself within the gender paradigm and even polices its linguistic boundaries. It is a sad paradox that a movement centered on the rights of women has led us to this curious juncture where the very definition of "woman" is under fierce dispute. How this happened is a strange story, rich in dramatic irony, and ultimately ruinous. The gender paradigm is feminism's offspring, and it has proven, as we will see, to be an Oedipal one.

Cosmos

Let me tell you a story.

In the beginning, there was water, and this water is where the gods are born. Two kinds of water: the turbulent feminine sea and the docile masculine river, fresh and saltwater intermingling, together forming a teeming pool from which the gods spring forth—all kinds of gods, noisy and raucous gods, gods who beget other gods. One of these gods arises as more powerful than the others, filled with a restless, conquering spirit. The watery orb of his origin becomes too small for him, too confining, and he decides to revolt. He gathers an army of monsters to do battle with the sea, his foremother, who has whipped herself into a terrifying frenzy, a primordial hurricane. He wins. He kills her. As an afterthought, he decides to make use of her corpse. He splits her down the middle, gutting her like a fish, and from her dead flesh forms the dome of the heavens and the sweep of the earth. He kills her consort as well, and from his blood, the warring god makes a multitude of tiny slaves whose sole purpose is to serve the gods, to keep them gratified and well fed.

This is the plot of the Enuma Elish, the Babylonian creation story. The race of slaves are human beings; the violent creator god is Marduk, and the divine feminine principle who births the pantheon is Tiamat. She cannot properly be called a god, because she is never an object of worship. There is never a temple or cult devoted to her, because human existence depends on her conquest. She is dead before the world begins.

Original Harmony

The first chapter of Genesis, which tells the biblical creation story, dates to the era of the Babylonian exile, when the Hebrew people were scattered, deprived of a temple, and living as refugees among their conquerors. The Enuma Elish was the dominant creation narrative of the time and provided the backdrop against which Genesis 1 was written. The Hebrew word *tehom*, typically translated as "the deep" over which the spirit of God hovers, is a cognate of the Akkadian word *tiamat*. However, as Genesis unfolds, it becomes clear that these two cosmologies could not be more different.

In the ancient mind, stories of origin are ultimately stories of identity and purpose. We cannot understand who we are and what we are made for without understanding where we come from. This is still true. There is an innate human tendency to seek out our origins to better understand ourselves. This is why, in order to fully inhabit a Christian sense of reality, we should begin at the beginning, with a careful look at Genesis. To better understand Genesis, we should read Genesis against its Babylonian foil, the Enuma Elish.

Both stories begin with chaos, but chaos of different kinds. The chaos of the Enuma Elish is noisy, violent, driven by conflicts between various gods. The chaos of Genesis is a tranquil emptiness; there are no other deities, no sense of conflict or violence. There is simply a void that God has come to fill, a *nothing* that God will replace with *something*.

Marduk, the Babylonian creator god, has his own origin story. He is the product of two divine beings, the progenitors of the gods, who have both been killed by the time Marduk creates the cosmos. The God of Genesis has no parents; he does not come into being. This absence of an origin testifies to his eternal presence. He is not *a* being, like Marduk, but Being itself, the infinite ground of all finite existence. He has nothing to prove, nothing to conquer, no need to establish his dominance. The oneness and sovereignty of God is strikingly opposed to the throngs of warring gods in the Enuma Elish.

Because there is no need to explain God's existence or his rise to power, Genesis 1 cuts straight to the main event: creation. In the Enuma Elish, the action of creation is secondary to the action of destruction. The creation of the world reads almost like an epilogue, buried in the text's final act. In Genesis, creation is the focal point. Creation is not an afterthought, the sudden impulse of a god who has satisfied his bloodlust. Creation, in Genesis, is intentional and orderly—a light flicking on in the dark. God doesn't create through violence and death, but through language; he speaks the world into being. This divine Word is the engine of creation, and it is this Word that will become incarnate in Christ.

There is no war in Genesis 1, only a productive tension between absence and presence, between something and nothing. Conflict and violence are not endemic to this reality; they do not enter the scene until later. Creation unfolds as an integral, interconnected whole: a cosmos. Each stage of this unfolding, each nested layer, is pronounced by God as *good*. There's a subtle sense of momentum as the narrative builds, each creative interval increasing in beauty and complexity, reaching an apex with the creation of human beings. These beings do not carry the bloodguilt of a fallen god; they bear the image of their Creator. They are not made to be slaves; they are tasked with tending the earth and filling it with life. The Genesis cosmology bestows upon human beings an exclusive kind of dignity, a dignity rooted in their roles as image bearers. Moreover, Genesis recognizes the duality of humankind, male and female; this difference is part of the goodness of creation, and both sexes share fully in the divine image and the commission to tend the earth. There is no sense here of hierarchy *between* male and female, but rather a shared, benevolent governance over the rest of creation.

The Enuma Elish has nothing to say about women specifically. The text deems the sexual duality of human beings unremarkable. It is worth noting that the central narrative conflict in the Enuma Elish is the war between Marduk and Tiamat: a masculine god and his foremother, a feminine power that must be violently subdued before creation can take place. This gendered conquest is utterly absent from Genesis 1. Between male and female there is no war, only a common dignity and a joint commission.

When we consider the first chapter of Genesis against the backdrop of the Enuma Elish, the distinctive emphases of Genesis are revealed in sharp relief: The reality we inhabit is a divinely created order, a harmonious cosmos. This order is *good*, intentionally and patiently called into being by an uncreated Creator. Human beings, male and female, are endowed with a unique dignity, marked by the image of their Creator, and entrusted with the sacred work of cultivating life. Sexual difference is not an extraneous or faulty feature of the cosmos but an essential part of its goodness.

The following chapters of Genesis further amplify this elevation of sexual difference. There are actually two cosmologies in Genesis. The first chapter describes creation

from a transcendent vantage point, a God's-eye view, as if
the narrator is suspended above the universe and watching
things flash into existence from afar. The second chapter of Genesis zooms in, way in. The narrator brings us
down into the dust of Eden, into an earthly paradise situated at the head of four rivers. God is depicted in bodily
terms, walking and talking with the first humans in a lush
garden. While the first cosmology emphasizes God's transcendence, the second shows us his intimacy. These two
accounts, taken together, reveal that the transcendent God
of Genesis 1 is also a deeply personal God, who desires
communion with his creatures. The two Genesis cosmologies are clearly distinct, but they are complementary rather
than contradictory; they describe the same event from two
angles, thus unveiling a bit more of God's ultimate mystery
and the primordial traces of our genesis.

Remember, ancient cosmologies must not be read
as literal history or science. To do so imposes a modern
mindset on premodern texts and obscures the truths the
stories seek to disclose. Creation accounts do not provide
scientific truths about material origins; they reveal deeper
truths: truths about *identity*—who God is and who we
are—and *purpose*, the ends for which we are made. Reading the creation narratives in Genesis and expecting to find
science, as I was raised to do, will make the two accounts
seem contradictory, forcing a reader to do mental gymnastics to reconcile them somehow or to reject them as false.
If these texts are instead read as divinely revealed poetry
and allegory—as *true myth*—a fuller picture of God, reality,
and the human person emerges.

The second creation account cuts almost immediately
to the creation of the first human being. God forms the
human (the *ādām*) from the humus of the soil and breathes
into his body, animating him with the divine breath of life.

This imagery reveals an important truth about our nature: we are both earth and breath, matter and spirit. We are physical creatures; our bodies are integral to who we are. Yet we are not *merely* matter, because God's breath enlivens each of us with an immaterial soul. This is one of the foundational principles of a Christian anthropology: every human being is a unity of body and soul.[1]

Then something unexpected happens. God looks at his creation, and instead of echoing the refrain from Genesis 1, he says the opposite words for the first time: it is *not good* that this human being is solitary, one of a kind. The human needs a counterpart, a companion. So begins one of my favorite passages: the parade of animals. God gets busy shaping and molding all kinds of creatures and presenting each before the human to "see what he would call them".[2] There's something comical about this imagery: here comes God with a monkey, a sheep, a gopher, a parrot; the *ādām* scopes it out, shakes his head, declares a name, and the misfit pageant continues, as if God and the *ādām* are playing a protracted game of Memory, but the cards never match.

Eventually, God goes back to the drawing board. Time for a new approach. He puts the human into a deep sleep, and from one of his ribs, God forms the first woman and presents her to the *ādām*. John Paul II reads this sleep as a sleep of nonbeing—God takes the first human out of existence entirely and brings two new beings into existence: man and woman.[3] He replaces the non-sexed, solitary humanity with a humanity that is differentiated into two modes of being human.

---

[1] For a concise account of Christian anthropology, see *The Catechism of the Catholic Church*, nos. 362–68 (hereafter cited as *CCC*).

[2] Genesis 2:19.

[3] John Paul II, "The Original Unity of Man and Woman", General Audience (November 7, 1979).

The *ādām*, who can now properly be called a *man*, issues a cry of wonder upon seeing the woman for the first time: "At last!" Listen to the delight and relief in those two words: "At last!" He immediately recognizes, in the silent declaration of her body, that she is both like him—more like him than any other earthly creature— and not like him. Their difference is complementary, but asymmetrical; this is not a mirror image or polar opposite. She resembles him in their shared humanity—"bone of my bones and flesh of my flesh"—but differs in the feminine form of her humanity. Genesis affirms a balance of sameness and difference between the sexes. This is a delicate balance that is difficult, but necessary, to maintain. Most theories of gender lose this balance, veering into extremes of uniformity (men and women are interchangeable) or polarity (men are from Mars, women are from Venus). Both extremes lose the fruitful tension expressed here in Genesis.

The opening act of this second cosmology could be read as an origin story of sexual difference itself, proclaiming that our identities as men and women *matter*; they carry sacred significance and occupy a prominent place in this worldview. To provide another contrasting example from the ancient world, Plato's *Timaeus*, a philosophical cosmology, only mentions women at the tail end of an extensive tour of the cosmos. When the *Timaeus* does mention them, it becomes clear that everything said previously in the text about human beings has applied to men only, because there are no women in the first generation of humankind. According to the *Timaeus*, men who live cowardly and unjust lives are reborn as women or other kinds of animals. Sexual difference, then, is not a purposeful feature of Plato's cosmos, but a defect, a bug. For Plato, any difference must be ranked hierarchically;

if men and women are different, one sex must be closer to the divine than the other. All of Plato's dialogues, in fact, privilege bonds between men, a common feature of many ancient texts: think of Gilgamesh and Enkidu, Achilles and Patroclus, and Aristotle's account of friendship between male peers.

Genesis, in contrast, uniquely foregrounds the importance of the male-female relationship, and this is a relationship not of domination, but of reciprocity. There is no hierarchy of value, no dynamic of superiority and inferiority. Sexual differentiation is not a mishap, but cause for celebration and wonder. This difference is *good*, our bodies are *good*, and both of these are an integral part of the created order, which is *good*. The emergence of man and woman from the sleep of nonbeing is not a footnote in our origin story: it's the ecstatic culmination.

There is more, if we dig deeper still. Genesis 2 emphasizes another vital principle: *the body reveals the person*. Our bodies are the visible reality through which we manifest our hidden, inner life. Each person's existence is entirely unrepeatable, and our unique personhood can only be made known to others through the frame of our embodiment. This sacramentality is displayed in the man's immediate recognition of the woman. They have not yet spoken; she has not verbally introduced herself. Her *body* speaks the truth of her identity, and this truth is immediately recognized by the man, who is struck with joy and wonder at the revelation of a person with whom he can—*at last!*—have true communion. Our bodies, then, serve a sacramental function, by revealing and communicating a spiritual reality. To use John Paul's words, "the body, in fact, and only the body, is capable of making visible what is invisible: the spiritual and the divine. It has been created to transfer into the visible reality of the world the mystery hidden from eternity in God, and thus to be a sign of it."[4]

It is not good for the human to be alone. This lacuna in the created order is mended not by the formation of more generic human beings or by male bonding, but by sexual differentiation. Sexual difference is a particular kind of difference because it is a difference that is arranged purposefully to correspond to the difference of the other. We are not talking about superficial differences here, like hair or eye color. We are talking about a body that is designed to fit another kind of body, in an entirely unique way. Maleness points toward femaleness, and vice versa. Our sexed body signals our inherent capacity and need for interpersonal communion.

There are all kinds of differences among human beings: differences in size, temperament, gifts, complexion. These differences can help create fruitful and vibrant relationships and communities. Only sexual difference, however, is capable of bringing another human being into existence. The one-flesh union between man and woman is not exclusive, facing inward and closed off to others. Rather, it is expansive and open, because this union alone has the potential to create new life. Communion and procreation: this is the twofold potential that is recognized and celebrated in the Genesis text through the man's cry of wonder.

Our bodies simultaneously proclaim our individual personhood and our capacity for relation. John Paul II, in his interpretation of Genesis, refers to this as "the spousal meaning of the body".[5] This does not indicate a merely

[4]John Paul II, *Man and Woman He Created Them: A Theology of the Body*, trans. Michael Waldstein (Ann Arbor: University of Michigan, 2006), 203.

[5]John Paul II, *Man and Woman*, 189.

biological reality but includes and expands beyond the capacity to procreate. The full spousal meaning of the body, outwardly declared by our visible sex characteristics, is the power to express love, to give oneself fully in love to another. This is the true *telos* or purpose of the human being: to become a *reciprocal gift*, to give love and receive it in turn. In our original condition, this self-gift is entirely free, not hindered or distorted by selfishness or domination. That is why the man and the woman are initially able to be naked before one another without shame. This signals their interior freedom, their reciprocal love that is free from corruption.

Before we move on from this discussion of man and woman in their original condition (spoiler: things quickly go awry), I want to make a final point about language. Both of the Genesis cosmologies depict a particular relationship between language and reality. In the first account, God uses language to create the cosmos *ex nihilo*: he draws order and being out of nothingness. In the second account, the man uses language to name what God creates. Divine speech makes reality; human speech identifies reality.

In the parade of animals, the man's act of naming does not impose meaning but recognizes meaning that objectively exists. God creates the animal and presents it to the man, who discerns its distinct nature and bestows a name that proclaims that nature. This dynamic is most obvious in the naming of woman. The man recognizes that the woman shares his nature, but in a modality that is distinct from his own. She is simultaneously like and unlike him. He chooses a word that corresponds to that two-fold reality: *ishshah* ("woman"), a word that includes *ish* ("man") while adding something new. These terms, man and woman, first appear in the text during this climactic encounter. Prior to this moment, the man is called the *ādām*. This, then, is a moment of *mutual* recognition; the man is both naming woman and renaming himself; it is through encountering her nature that he is able truly to understand his own. Throughout this account, naming is depicted as a linguistic response to that which is being named. Reality, then, exists prior to our naming it, and our language is true and meaningful when it corresponds to what exists.

The understanding of language portrayed in Genesis contrasts starkly with the view that dominates contemporary debates about gender. Most gender theories hold that what we think of as "reality" is a linguistic and social construction. Our use of the words "woman" and "man", so this theory goes, creates the illusion that sex is a binary. We will discuss this perspective in more detail in subsequent chapters. For now, I merely want to point out that the constructionist view of language is a complete inversion of the correspondence view depicted in Genesis. In this divinely revealed origin story, our language does not project meaning onto things. Rather, meaning intrinsically exists in what God creates. Moreover, this meaning is intelligible to us, and language, a mark of God's image in us, enables human beings to proclaim that inherent meaning.

Thus far, the Genesis cosmology has given us a vivid picture of humankind in our original condition. We are part of a created order, a harmonious whole, that is brought into being and held in existence by a loving Creator. We are unities of body and spirit; our bodies are an integral part of our identity that connect us to the created order and serve as a bridge between our inmost being and the outer world, and a sacramental sign of the hidden mystery of God. Both man and woman are made in God's image, and our sexual difference is part of the goodness of the created order, signaling that we are made for reciprocal love. We have been granted a share in the divine power of language in order to make words that reveal the truth about ourselves and our world.

Harmony, order, communion: these are the key features of our prelapsarian state. But we have reached a turning point in the narrative; the balanced relationship between man and woman is about to undergo a radical transformation. There is a clear rupture between human nature in the original condition and human nature corrupted by sin. Genesis addresses both dimensions of our origin and identity: who we were created to be and who we have unfortunately become.

Original Schism

The best lies are not outright falsehoods but subtle distortions of the truth. The most effective temptations are those that take hold of a genuine desire for something good and twist that desire toward a false or lesser good. So it is with the woman and the serpent. "You will be like God", he promises. These words lead her away from the recognition that she already bears a likeness to God; she is a living, breathing image of God in the visible world. The words of the serpent, as John Paul II writes, cause doubt to well up in the human heart, doubt about "the goodness of the gift": the gift of creation, the gift of our bodies, the gift of divine grace that raises us out of a purely natural state and into a dynamic of communion with God.[6]

Sometimes this moment is described as the moment when "sin entered the world". This wording makes sin sound like a substance, like some kind of metaphysical tar

---

[6]John Paul II, *Man and Woman*, 236.

that coats and sullies the soul. But sin is not a *something*; it is a *nothing*, an absence. That is why this moment is known as the Fall. Athanasius, an influential early Church father and bishop, provides an interpretation of the Fall in his treatise *On the Incarnation*. Athanasius writes that human beings are made of matter, and thus we are finite and prone to disease, decay, and death. That is our natural state. Because God had mercy upon us and desired for us to share in his eternal life, he granted us, in the beginning, "a further gift", a "share in the power of his own Word", that we may be able to "abide in blessedness".[7] The original state of man and woman described in Genesis, then, is a supranatural one; they were lifted out of their mortal state by a gift of divine grace. When the first humans broke faith with God, this grace was lost, and humankind "fell" into mortality, becoming subject to death. The fall is not a plunge from our natural state into a more corrupt, unnatural state: it is a fall from what the Catechism calls "the grace of original holiness", a reversion to our mortal condition.[8]

Some interpreters, perhaps most famously Milton in *Paradise Lost*, have made much of the fact that the serpent tempts the woman, using this as justification to portray women as weak and morally compromised, gateways to sin. But a Catholic interpretation has to take the long view, reading this story in the arc of salvation history. From that perspective, one can see a similitude between the narrative of the Fall and the Annunciation, when Mary is approached by a divine messenger. From the early Church Fathers onward, Catholic interpreters have recognized this parallel between Eve and Mary. Philosopher-saint Edith Stein puts

---

[7] Saint Athanasius, *On the Incarnation* (Yonkers, NY: St Vladimir's Seminary Press, 2011), 52.

[8] *CCC* 399.

it this way: "As woman was the first to be tempted, so did God's message of grace come first to a woman, and each time woman's assent determined the destiny of humanity as a whole."[9] The woman's temptation indicates not her weakness, but rather her influence: woman's assent has the power to shape and reshape humankind.

The first consequence of eating the forbidden fruit is a sudden awareness of nakedness and an impulse to hide from one another. This harkens back to the concluding verse of the second creation account: "the man and his wife were both naked, and were not ashamed." Now, something has soured, something has gone wrong. Their naked bodies, once a source of wonder and joy, elicit discomfort and shame. Not only do the man and the woman hide from one another; they also hide themselves from the presence of God. Conflict has disrupted the original harmony; shame has corrupted the original intimacy. Self-gift has become self-erasure.

In his writings on the theology of the body, John Paul II draws out the many layers of meaning that are packed into this moment. The sudden impulse to hide is a sharp contrast from the man's free and full participation in the "visibility of the world" that is depicted earlier in the text.[10] The man and the woman now seek to hide their sexually differentiated bodies, obscuring the sacramental symbolism expressed by that difference. According to John Paul II, this moment is "the collapse of the original acceptance of the body as a sign of the person in the visible world."[11] We have lost sight of the truth that to see a *body* is to see a *person*, a person made in the image of God. Moreover,

[9] Edith Stein, *Essays on Woman* (Washington, D.C.: ICS Publications, 1987), 63.

[10] John Paul II, *Man and Woman*, 175.

[11] John Paul II, *Man and Woman*, 242.

the man and the woman have lost the sense of the image of God in *themselves*, not just in the other. Shame is a turning away, a "detachment from love".[12] The original union of the man and the woman, their "serene community of love", has ended.[13]

This outer rupture in the relationship between man and woman indicates an inner rupture in the human person's very being. Sin has fractured the call to unity between the sexes and has also created a fracture in the original spiritual-somatic unity of the individual. There is now a war within that threatens the wholeness of the human person. The body becomes a "hotbed of resistance against the spirit", no longer feeling integral to the self, but something that must be tamed and controlled.[14] This state of interior discord is *concupiscence*, and it brings about "difficulty in identifying oneself with one's own body"—and also, I would argue, in recognizing the sacred personhood of other bodies.[15] Concupiscence depersonalizes the human person, making him an object for the other and an object for himself. The body in particular is objectified, becoming a "terrain of appropriation".[16]

When God confronts the man and woman about what they've done, their reaction is to equivocate, to cast blame elsewhere, to subtly twist the truth—just like the serpent. Language itself has been perverted; words are now being used to obfuscate and manipulate reality, rather than to reveal what is true. In the original Hebrew, man's response to God's question features a curious doubling of the verb: *the woman whom you gave to me gave me the fruit and I ate*

---

[12] John Paul II, *Man and Woman*, 249.
[13] Stein, *Essays on Woman*, 61.
[14] John Paul II, *Man and Woman*, 244.
[15] John Paul II, *Man and Woman*, 249.
[16] John Paul II, *Man and Woman*, 260.

it. This doubling emphasizes the notion of *gift* and subtly rejects the gift of the woman, a gift the man wholeheartedly and joyfully celebrated just a few verses earlier. His response to God casts doubt on the goodness of God's gifts—particularly the gift of woman—just as the woman's acquiescence to the serpent reflects a distrust in the original goodness of her own nature.

While misogynist interpreters prefer to perseverate on the woman's role in the Fall, the sacred text resists this reading, again and again stressing man and woman's shared condition. In the beginning, *both* are created in the image of God; *both* are given dominion over the earth and the mission to make it fruitful; *both* are naked and unashamed. In the narrative of the Fall, *both* are present to hear the tempter's words; *both* take and eat the fruit; *both* experience a sudden and shameful awareness of nakedness; *both* hide from each other and from God; *both* twist the truth to cast blame; *both* suffer the consequences of sin. The text never paints one sex as the villain or the victim.

In the midst of all this mirroring, there are meaningful asymmetries. The original goodness and the subsequent evil are fully shared, but the consequences carry different implications for each sex. To the woman, God says: "your desire shall be for your husband, and he shall rule over you." The man's response to the woman's desire is to dominate her, which "makes an object out of a human being".[17] The dynamic of communion is displaced by a dynamic of possession; mutual love between persons becomes a utilitarian exchange between person and object. Edith Stein's description of this new order is quite pointed: "The relationship of the sexes since the Fall has become a brutal relationship of master and slave.... Man uses her as

---

[17]John Paul II, *Man and Woman*, 252.

a means to achieve his own ends in the exercise of his
work or in pacifying his own lust."[18] John Paul II writes
that "the relationship of the gift changes into a relationship of appropriation", and while this appropriation is
mutual and not totally one-sided, it happens "more at the
woman's expense".[19] For John Paul, the man has a special
responsibility as "guardian of the reciprocity of the gift".[20]
Maintaining the balance of the gift is entrusted to both
sexes, but it depends more on the man whether the balance is kept or violated.

I want to underscore that the dynamic of domination is
not God's intention for men and women, but a distortion
due to sin. While the serpent and the ground are explicitly
cursed, the man and the woman are not. God's words here
are a foretelling, a description of consequences that will
unfold as a result of losing the grace of original holiness.
Human nature is now marked by concupiscence, an inner
conflict between body and spirit. The Protestant understanding regards concupiscence itself as sinful, and human
nature after the Fall as utterly depraved. The Catholic
vision is more optimistic: our nature is *wounded*, not completely corrupt. The human heart is a "battlefield between
love and concupiscence", but the battle is not yet lost.[21]

Redemption of the Gift

In the Gospel of Matthew, when Jesus is questioned by the
Pharisees about whether divorce is permissible, he refers
back to Genesis, to the original order of creation: "Have

[18] Stein, *Essays on Woman*, 71.
[19] John Paul II, *Man and Woman*, 260–61.
[20] John Paul II, *Man and Woman*, 260–61.
[21] John Paul II, *Man and Woman*, 260–61.

you not read that he who made them from the beginning
made them male and female, and said, 'For this reason a
man shall leave his father and mother and be joined to
his wife, and the two shall become one'? So they are no
longer two but one."[22] The Pharisees quickly counter that
the Mosaic law permitted divorce, allowing men to "put
away" their wives for any cause. Christ draws a sharp distinction between this law, which is part of the order corrupted by sin, and God's original intention for men and
women. In the fallen order, sin has hardened the hearts of
men and women toward one another, but, to use Christ's
words, "from the beginning it was not so."

Christ's turn toward Genesis is a significant move. He
does not appeal to the law when confronted with questions about how men and women should relate to one
another. He appeals to *cosmology*, to the sacred narratives of
Genesis that give an account of our identity and purpose as
human beings. Genesis still speaks the truth about men and
women, about who we are created to be. Christ's Incarnation, his coming into the world, ushers in a new order,
the order of grace and redemption, that seeks to restore
what has been broken by sin. Christ does not direct us to
structure our relationships according to our "hardness of
heart".[23] He turns our eyes back toward Genesis and urges
us, with divine help, to reclaim the goodness of the created
order, the gift of our bodies and the earth, and to cultivate
anew a dynamic of reciprocity between the sexes.

Edith Stein, in her writings about men and women,
draws on Genesis and the Gospels to argue that "the Lord
clearly declared the new kingdom of God would bring a
new order of relationship between the sexes, i.e., it would
put an end to the relationships caused by the Fall and

---

[22] Matthew 19:4–6.
[23] Matthew 19:8.

would restore the original order."[24] Sacred Scripture, taken as a whole, highlights three states of identity and relation between the sexes. There is the original order, described in the first two chapters of Genesis. In this order, sexual difference is understood and experienced as *gift*, as a source of fruitfulness and love. There is a dynamic balance between sameness and difference, and the man and the woman have a shared commission—a common mission—to generate life and govern the earth. Once the man and the woman break faith with God, a fracture heaves through all of creation: through the center of the human person, through the bond between man and woman, through the connection between humankind and the earth. In this fallen order, the human person is now at war with himself, and this inner conflict erupts outward, pushing the equilibrium between the sexes into a swinging pendulum of conflict and domination. Difference, no longer recognized as gift, is understood as opposition. The final, redemptive order seeks to correct this opposition. This order begins with Mary's assent to become the Mother of God Incarnate. She is the new Eve. Her *yes* to God untwists the knot of Eve's *no*. The redemptive order harkens back to the beginning, to restore the original justice of creation through the engine of grace. Grace has the power to heal our wounded nature, to soften the hardness of our hearts, and to restore the broken covenants between God and humanity and between woman and man.

†

We live now as exiles, driven from Eden into the wilderness. In this wilderness, there is a continual "struggle between the sexes, one pitted against the other, as they

---

[24] Stein, *Essays on Woman*, 63.

fight for their rights and, in doing so, no longer appear to hear the voices of nature and of God."[25] We are born into this fallen order, but the realm of redemption remains open to us, beckoning. Feminism rightly recognizes that something is amiss, that the relationship between men and women has been too often characterized by domination. However, blind to the dimension of grace, the solutions offered by its theories are themselves caught in the fallen forces of conflict, in the continual grasping for power over others.

A Christian approach is one that seeks to move from the wilderness of sin and into the realm of grace, all the while remaining attentive to the voice of nature and the voice of God. This means taking Genesis seriously, regarding it as "true myth", as a divinely revealed cosmology that describes our origin so as to give an enduring account of our identity and purpose as human beings, as woman and man. Within this redemptive order, we can recover our wonder. We can recognize anew the abundance of *the gift*—the gift of our bodies, the gift of our shared humanity, and the gift of our sexual difference.

---

[25] Stein, *Essays on Woman*, 76.

Waves

I last taught Gender Theory in the fall of 2016, for what would turn out to be the final time. After my harsh awakening the previous year, I was teaching it differently than I'd taught it before. Instead of assembling a list of readings from within the canon of feminist and gender theory, I structured the course as an exploration of two paradigms: the Christian paradigm and the gender paradigm. I assigned Christian philosophers of gender such as Elizabeth Fox-Genovese, Prudence Allen, and Gertrud von le Fort, writers who would *never* appear on a standard gender studies reading list. To represent the feminist perspective, I chose figures of towering influence, like Simone de Beauvoir and Judith Butler, whose ideas continue to drive feminist and gender theory today. I tried to get my students to view the gender paradigm from a distance—rather than blindly entering it—in order to be able to see its foundational premises.

This all sounds fine in concept. In practice, things were a bit messy. The class was a mix of ardent ideologues who had already fled Christianity for the far reaches of gender theory; a moderate middle who were trying to inhabit both Christianity and feminism; and one or two devout Christians who wanted to understand what all the fuss was about. The radical fringe was by far the most vocal, and most of our seminars devolved into bouts of Socratic sparring, as I tried to prod at their assumptions and tease out subtle contradictions.

This proved difficult. Those students were not interested in following a line of argument. Instead, they would adeptly pivot from one talking point to the next, ducking and rolling away from any probing questions. Once during a discussion about abortion, I was asking the students whether or not abortion ends the life of a human being. The vocal students dodged that question entirely, going immediately on the offensive, arguing that Christians had no right to make moral judgments about abortion, because of Christianity's historical complicity in war and violence. While that pronouncement is certainly worth discussing, it did not at all track with the argument we were evaluating. This was a typical move in those seminars, and I could never tell if it was an intentional strategy or if these students were truly unable to follow and evaluate a single line of reasoning. Either way, it disrupted my attempt to play the role of a placid, noble Socrates, gently nudging his eager student-ducklings toward truth. The reality was far more exasperating, like flailing around in a murky pond, trying to catch an eel with my bare hands.

Nonetheless, there were some "aha!" moments over the semester—moments when a well-aimed point hit the mark and I could see a flash of realization in my students' eyes, a glimmer of insight. One of these occurred during a discussion about Christian feminism. I asked the students how many of them identified as a Christian feminist. Over half the class responded in the affirmative. I then asked those students to define Christian feminism. One by one, they did, each offering an iteration of the idea that men and women are equal, some adding the extra layer of overturning patriarchal oppression. "Interesting", I said, when they had finished. "Not one of you mentioned Christ." The students exchanged guilty smiles. They recognized, in that instant, that there was nothing particularly

Christian in their definitions of feminism. This confirmed my working hypothesis, the suspicion around which I had structured the course: Christianity and contemporary feminism operate from different foundational assumptions about reality, and most versions of Christian feminism have their roots in the feminist worldview rather than the Christian one. So-called "Christian feminism" is, too often, secular feminism with a light Jesus glaze on top, a cherry-picked biblical garnish.

Feminism: A Bird's-Eye View

The previous chapter explored the canopy of the Christian paradigm, as revealed in our origin story. Now, I would like to begin the work of exploring the gender paradigm by describing its progenitor: twentieth-century feminism. As noted in the opening chapter, the gender paradigm is the Oedipal offspring of feminism—*offspring* because it is through feminist theory that the concept of gender has taken hold of our cultural imagination, and *Oedipal* because like Oedipus' murder of his own father, this concept has eroded the very foundation of feminism, turning "woman" into an identity that can be freely appropriated by men, regardless of material reality.

Before we begin, I need to make a concession. Readers who have some familiarity with feminist theory and history are no doubt sitting back dubiously at this point, arms crossed, wondering how I am going to pull this off—how I am going to give an account of "feminism", as if there is one coherent movement to describe.

This is a fair criticism, because it is more accurate to speak of *feminisms*, plural, than a monolithic *feminism*. There are almost endless varieties, a multitude of different camps: liberal feminism, Marxist feminism, psychoanalytic feminism, poststructuralist feminism, French feminism, Black feminism, sex-positive feminism, gender critical feminism—the list goes on. This diversity facilitates a rhetorical move I commonly see: deflecting any criticism of feminism by shrugging it off as "not *real* feminism". This is a lapse into the "no true Scotsman" fallacy, using the vast array of feminisms to duck any generalized critiques.

I also regularly hear the phrase "radical feminism" bandied about, which never seems affixed to any one group. Some Catholics deem any pro-abortion feminist "radical". In feminist studies, "radical feminists" refers to 1970s lesbian separatists who formed all-women communes in order to live independently from men. For today's transgender activists, anyone who holds the common-sense view that a male human being can't be a woman is the "radical" one. Rather than naming a specific group within feminism, "radical feminism" has apparently become a way to signal the kind of feminism one doesn't like.

To further complicate matters, not only are there many versions of feminism within the thin slice of our contemporary moment, but there are even more varieties when we look at feminism over time, from the beginning of the twentieth century until today.

Feminism as a term first began to circulate in Europe at the end of the nineteenth century, making its way across the Atlantic by 1910. The history of feminism is typically characterized as having several distinct "waves", with the first wave erupting in the movement for women's suffrage. Prior to the first wave, women were generally not granted the right to vote, to own property, to serve on juries or be witnesses in court, to have custodial rights over their own children, to stand for election, or to attend most colleges and universities.

In America, the movement for women's rights grew out of the movement to abolish slavery. Prominent leaders such as Elizabeth Cady Stanton, Susan B. Anthony, and Sojourner Truth were active in both movements, as well as former slave Frederick Douglass, who attended the first women's rights convention in Seneca Falls, New York, in 1848.

Early feminism also had significant ties to the Temperance Movement to ban alcohol. Women and children in this era were the primary victims of rampant alcohol-related domestic abuse, and it was around this cause that women first organized large coalitions, such as the Women's Christian Temperance Union. Their efforts to advocate for legislative change were temporarily successful during the thirteen-year period of Prohibition. The struggle for women's suffrage proved even more victorious, with the passing of the Nineteenth Amendment to the Constitution in 1920, which guaranteed women the right to vote.

First-wave feminists, for the most part, were not radicals or revolutionaries. Most were middle-class wives and mothers, committed Christians who opposed abortion. Their aim was not to overthrow or subvert the system but to gain legal representation within it. After that goal was achieved, the feminist movement more or less disbanded. There was not, at this time, the idea of an all-pervasive patriarchy that needed to be continually contested. That is why the feminist movement is described as having distinct "waves": there was a long, thirty-year interval between the passing of the Nineteenth Amendment and feminism's second wave, which erupted in the late 1960s.

During this interval, a major event occurred: the Second World War. Most able-bodied men were drafted as soldiers, and in their absence, women supported the war effort by working in factories and shipyards, as well as serving various roles in the Women's Army Auxiliary Corps. Think of Rosie the Riveter, that iconic image of a woman in a polka-dotted kerchief and coveralls, flexing under the slogan *We Can Do It!* By 1945, women comprised 37% of the US workforce, and a quarter of married women were employed outside the home. This was a massive cultural shift, one that would prove impossible to roll back, even when the war ended and men returned home.

In 1963, Betty Friedan wrote *The Feminine Mystique*, a book that became a catalyst for the resurgence of feminism. Friedan's aim was to draw back the curtain of the glowing, golden 1950s housewife to expose "the problem that has no name": women's deep and listless unhappiness when confined to domestic roles. This book was a hit, and the Women's Liberation Movement caught fire, one of many movements for social change in the late 1960s. The unifying goal of this movement was not just legal equality, but broader social and political equality, as second-wave feminists began to actively rethink women's roles within the home and in the workforce.

A major part of this effort was a renewed emphasis on so-called "reproductive freedom"—that is, unlimited access to birth control and abortion. First-wave feminists generally opposed abortion, seeing no inherent conflict between their rights and the rights of their unborn children. Initially, second-wave feminists were divided on the abortion issue, until the male-led National Association for the Repeal of Abortion Law (NARAL) forged an alliance with the newly formed National Organization for Women (NOW).[1] This alliance between feminism

---

[1] See Sue Ellen Browder, *Subverted: How I Helped the Sexual Revolution Hijack the Women's Movement* (San Francisco: Ignatius Press, 2015).

and the pro-abortion movement would prove to be long-lasting; the right to *ad libitum* abortion is now the central and immovable plank of the mainstream feminist platform.

By most accounts, this second wave lasted for about two decades, until the feminist movement devolved into the "sex wars" of the 1980s, an internal conflict between feminists who opposed pornography and prostitution as forces of female oppression, and the so-called "sex-positive" feminists who viewed these as liberating. The third wave of feminism that emerged from this conflict in the 1990s was similarly preoccupied with sexual politics and tended to toe the sex-positive line, emphasizing uninhibited sexual freedom. During this wave, consent became the lone benchmark for sex to be considered licit. If a woman chooses a particular sex act, that sex act is good, even if it involves prostitution, pornography, or sadomasochism. In the early 1990s, Anita Hill's testimony cast a spotlight on the problem of sexual harassment in the broader culture, underscoring the importance of female consent, and in the academy, theorist Judith Butler rolled out her influential notion of gender as a socially compelled performance. This idea quickly trickled down to the level of popular culture, and indeed there is something self-consciously edgy and performative about third-wave feminism—think Riot Grrrl punk music and SlutWalk marches. The emphasis on individual choice and freedom is a key marker of third-wave feminism, which tended to adopt a postmodern sensibility, emphasizing diversity among women and ironically playing with gender norms and expectations.

With the turn of the millennium, the feminist movement migrated online, gaining renewed prominence through popular blogs and social media. This reshaped feminism yet again, into what many call a fourth wave, beginning around 2012. One can see in this new iteration a growing ambivalence toward unrestrained sexual license, an emerging awareness that women can be mistreated even within the boundaries of what is technically consensual. #MeToo and #BelieveAllWomen—these are the calling cards of fourth-wave feminism. This wave intensified many features of the third wave, such as a focus on diversity and the intersection of various forms of oppression, particularly racism and sexism. Even *more* embracing of gender plurality, fourth-wave feminism took the unprecedented step of rejecting the idea that a "woman", by definition, is a biological female. This move would have been inconceivable in first- and second-wave feminism. If third-wave feminism had a rebellious, libertarian, anticensorship vibe, fourth-wave feminists at times veer in the opposite direction, policing and prescribing codes of behavior and speech designed to reflect the latest gender trends.

Here we are, bobbing in the wake of the fourth wave. Although, to be honest, by now the metaphor has broken down. We no longer have a movement that ebbs and recedes, with interludes between distinct waves. We have a roiling ocean, fed by numerous streams—like Tiamat, the tumultuous sea goddess from the Enuma Elish, and her many squabbling progeny.

With that sketch of feminist history in the background, I'd like to take a closer look at three prominent philosophical currents that gave rise to the gender paradigm. I'm particularly interested in the underlying ideas that animate pop feminism—the feminism of memes, social media, and everyday conversation. I will not attempt to provide an exhaustive tour through the arcane corners of ivory tower feminism. Rather, I want to trace several streams that have filtered down into popular rhetoric and now shape our cultural notions of gender. Each of these currents, I would argue, reflects an implicit worldview—a particular understanding of reality, the human person, and what it means to be free.

Existentialist Feminism

In my reading of American feminism, Simone de Beauvoir looms large. That may seem strange, considering that de Beauvoir is not American at all, but French, and her most famous work, *The Second Sex*, was written in 1949, a relatively quiet period for feminism, during that long interval between the first and second waves. Even so, de Beauvoir was the first philosopher to give an account of male domination that pervades all spheres of human life and thought. The very concept of "woman", she argues, is figured as an object, slave, or "other" to man, and female human beings are socialized to conform to this understanding of womanhood from birth. This idea is behind her well-known line, "One is not born, but rather becomes, a woman."[2] That statement is the mustard seed of gender theory.

The Second Sex is de Beauvoir's attempt to give an account of how the idea of woman as "other" came to be, and the result is a sweeping eight-hundred-page treatise that draws alternately, and selectively, from philosophy, biology, history, anthropology, psychoanalysis, religion, and literature. This book had a profound influence on Betty Friedan, whose own bestseller ignited the keg of the 1960s women's movement. Via Friedan, de Beauvoir's account of domesticity and female biology as domains of enslavement shaped the ideology and goals of second-wave feminism, and, I would argue, continue to frame the feminist approach to abortion and motherhood today.

[2] Simone de Beauvoir, *The Second Sex* (New York: Vintage, 2011), 283.

At times, it is difficult to discern whether de Beauvoir is writing in a descriptive or prescriptive mode, but even her descriptions are value-laden and explicitly grounded in an existentialist framework, which she establishes in her introduction. Existentialism, a school of philosophy, receives its name from one of its central claims: the idea that *existence precedes essence*. Essence, in philosophical lingo, refers to the "whatness" of a thing, a stable nature that defines what something is. In the previous chapter, we discussed the Christian view of the human person as a body-soul unity, which is one understanding of what a human being *essentially* is. Discussions of "human nature" are implicitly essentialist, because they are concerned with defining a shared, underlying essence common to all human beings. The traditional philosophical position is that *essence precedes existence*. In other words, what a human being *is* in its very nature is prior to the fact of my particular existence. Existentialism reverses this: I am not a human being by the mere fact that I exist; I must *become* a human being through my creative action in the world. Humanness becomes something I achieve, rather than something I am given.

In de Beauvoir's version of existentialism, a human being is an "autonomous freedom" that is in tension with its "facticity", its material and finite condition.[3] The human thus inhabits an "ambiguity of existence", caught in a "drama of flesh and spirit, of finitude and transcendence".[4] When I read de Beauvoir, I am reminded of the ancient Stoic philosophers, who saw human beings as emanations of the divine that are trapped in the fleshly prisons of bodies. Death, then, is an escape, a return to the divine *pneuma*, the God-Soul that pervades the cosmos. De

---

[3] De Beauvoir, *The Second Sex*, 16–17.
[4] De Beauvoir, *The Second Sex*, 763.

Beauvoir's existentialism, however, is atheistic. There is no *pneuma*, no God, no emanation. I am not a *soul* or divine spark trapped in a body; I am an infinite consciousness constrained by my biological and material circumstances. When de Beauvoir refers to *transcendence*, she is not alluding to God but speaking of the capacity for human beings to *transcend* the brute facts of their existence, through creative action. To fail to exercise this capacity for transcendence is to lapse into immanence, to relinquish our freedom and become subjected to our facticity as physical beings. If we consent to this "fall" from transcendence to immanence, it is a moral failing; if we inflict such a fall on another person, this is oppression. De Beauvoir considers each to be an "absolute evil".[5]

For de Beauvoir, there is no such thing as human nature, only the human condition, that state of tension or ambiguity between transcendence and immanence. There is no intrinsic meaning to the world or to our lives. Meaning must be made; it cannot simply be found. It is up to us to justify our existence, to give it purpose. We are not *created*; rather, we *create ourselves*, and failing to take up this work of self-creation is a moral transgression. To be clear, this is not lazy, libertine relativism: "Do whatever makes you happy!" De Beauvoir explicitly states that she is concerned not with what will make women happy, only with what will make them free.[6]

Reading *The Second Sex* is an odd experience. I find myself nodding my head in agreement and then, a paragraph later, shaking my head in disbelief, such as when she suggests that vomiting during pregnancy indicates a woman's unconscious rejection of her child. In all of

[5] De Beauvoir, *The Second Sex*, 16
[6] De Beauvoir, *The Second Sex*, 17.

her accounts of the various stages of a woman's life—childhood, puberty, adolescence, marriage, pregnancy, motherhood—she focuses on the negative, the ambivalent, the pathological. While there can certainly be a dark underside to all of these dimensions, I can't help but come away with the impression that she hates being female. She is right that what is traditionally masculine has been consistently valued more highly than what is associated with the feminine. Unfortunately, her underlying worldview perpetuates this same error.

Because de Beauvoir sets facticity at odds with freedom, and immanence in opposition to transcendence, women are oppressed not merely by social forces, but by their biology. Listen to how she describes the natural state of women: "to give birth and to breast-feed are not *activities* but natural functions; they do not involve a project, which is why the woman finds no motive there to claim a higher meaning for her existence; she passively submits to her biological destiny."[7] Now read her description of the primitive man: "Man's case is radically different. He does not provide for the group in the way worker bees do, by a simple vital process, but rather by acts that transcend his animal condition."[8] These are the phrases she uses to characterize the work of women in this passage: *condemned, lock[ed] into repetition and immanence, produces nothing new, prey to the species, riveted to her body like the animal.* Contrast those with her more vigorous account of man's work: *expands his grasp, conquers, constructs, appropriates, annexes; through such actions he tests his own power; he posits; he realizes himself; he opens up the future.*[9] She goes on to make the odd

[7] De Beauvoir, *The Second Sex*, 73.

[8] De Beauvoir, *The Second Sex*.

[9] De Beauvoir, *The Second Sex*, 73–74.

assertion that the inherent danger of man's activity endows
him with supreme dignity, because it is not "in giving life
but in risking his life that man raises himself above the animal."[10] She neglects altogether the fact that childbirth itself
is dangerous; giving life and risking life have, throughout
history, gone hand in hand for women as well.

This slant toward the masculine and away from the feminine remains consistent through the entire book. If I were
to sum up *The Second Sex* as an SAT analogy, it would be
thus: masculine is to transcendence as feminine is to immanence. I can imagine that trying to spear fish or tanning
hide or plowing a rocky furrow can at times be quite repet-
itive and even futile work. Yet it is only domestic labor that
she describes in this way, while giving masculine action an
exhilarating spin. Moreover, this bias is not accidental. It's a
feature of her worldview, rather than a bug. She writes that
a woman "finds the confirmation of masculine claims in the
core of her being" and that she "aspires to and recognizes
the values concretely attained by males."[11]

Simone de Beauvoir's account of the human condition puts a woman necessarily at war with herself, with
the given state of her embodiment. Woman is an absurdity; she is an autonomous freedom trapped in a body that
is designed to house an other. Her only hope is to fight
against her facticity, always—to become as much like a
man as possible. In order for a woman to create herself, she
must repudiate herself. She must recognize the feminine
as devoid of meaning and turn her gaze, her aspirations,
toward the masculine ideal.

De Beauvoir centers life's meaning on work and production. Because pregnancy, birth, and breastfeeding are

[10] De Beauvoir, *The Second Sex*, 74.
[11] De Beauvoir, *The Second Sex*, 74.

all natural functions, these cannot facilitate transcendence; a woman cannot transcend her facticity through motherhood into a higher plane of meaning. Man, on the other hand, is an autonomous and complete individual, because he is a producer: "his existence is justified by the work he provides."[12] She is explicit that "work alone can guarantee [woman's] concrete freedom."[13] It's difficult to read that line and not hear a fleeting echo of *Arbeit macht frei*, the Nazi slogan etched into the gateway to Auschwitz. Work will make you free.

In de Beauvoir's defense, however, she is not championing the hectic life of the female CEO who "leans in" to long work hours, constantly juggling a high-powered career with little semblance of a family life. She takes on the modern ideal of "having it all" in her chapter on the so-called independent woman of her day, with insights that continue to ring true nearly a century later. The modern woman, she argues, is not free, but divided. She is unable to escape the demands of the feminine world, even while jockeying to succeed in the masculine world. She has to live both like a man and like a woman, and "her workload and her fatigue are multiplied as a result."[14] De Beauvoir is thoroughly pessimistic about combining motherhood and a career. "Even one child is enough to entirely paralyze a woman's activity", she writes.[15]

Soon after I finished my Ph.D., I reached out to a former professor of mine, asking how she managed to have a successful academic career *and* multiple babies. I was not yet a mother, and the prospect of balancing that with academia seemed daunting. The professor's advice was

[12] De Beauvoir, *The Second Sex*, 440.
[13] De Beauvoir, *The Second Sex*, 721.
[14] De Beauvoir, *The Second Sex*, 725.
[15] De Beauvoir, *The Second Sex*, 735.

simple: Marry well. Having a supportive partner is everything. "It has been a wonderful experience for me", she
said, "and a nightmare for a friend of mine." The difference? She had a husband who shared the domestic work,
and her friend did not. This advice has proven true. In my
own marriage, there has never been the expectation that
child-rearing and home-making is my sole responsibility
as a woman—it is our shared vocation as a couple. Our
marital motto is a line from Homer's *Odyssey*: "No finer,
greater gift in the world than that, when man and woman
possess their home, two minds, two hearts that work as
one. Despair to their enemies, joy to all their friends. Their
own best claim to glory."[16]

This vision of a shared domestic sphere is not the solution advocated by de Beauvoir. Within her existentialist
framework, such a move would not make women free,
but would rather doom both women and men to immanence, to work that merely repeats and supports existence
rather than transcending it. For de Beauvoir, nothing less
than a Marxist revolution will do. True equality cannot
be achieved piecemeal, by tweaking a law here or custom
there: "the forest must be planted all at once."[17] Within
this newly cultivated realm, a girl could be raised with "the
same demands and honors, the same severity and freedom,
as her brothers." She would "prove her worth in work
and sports, actively rivalling the boys."[18] This is her vision
for women's emancipation, the one "promised", but not
realized, by the Soviet revolution:

> ... women raised and educated exactly like men would
> work under the same conditions and for the same salaries;

[16] Homer, *The Odyssey*, trans. Robert Fagles (New York: Penguin, 1997), 174.
[17] De Beauvoir, *The Second Sex*, 761.
[18] De Beauvoir, *The Second Sex*, 761.

erotic freedom would be accepted by custom ... women would be *obliged* to provide another livelihood for themselves; marriage would be based on a free engagement that the spouses could break when they wanted to; motherhood would be freely chosen—that is, birth control and abortion would be allowed—and in return all mothers and their children would be given the same rights; maternity leave would be paid for by the society that would have responsibility for the children.[19]

I'm all for paid maternity leave, but I can't help but wonder who would be employed with all the domestic drudgery in those state-run childcare centers—not de Beauvoir, presumably! One could try to argue that de Beauvoir is angling to abolish the polarized spheres of masculinity and femininity altogether, by establishing a neutral sphere that is neither. In one sense that is true: her aim is for an androgynous world. She argues that once girls are adopted from birth into the masculine sphere, that sphere will no longer be perceived as masculine, but as "androgynous".[20] Even in this final description of her ideal society, it is clear that it is not the men who are changing, but the women. The masculine standard remains in place, even if it is now rebranded as androgyny because women fully take part in it. Even if I let de Beauvoir have the last word, that word will reaffirm my point. She ends her lengthy tome about the predicament of women with a final call for men and women to "unequivocally affirm their *brotherhood*".[21]

We will dig into the ramifications of these ideas more in subsequent chapters. My purpose here is to highlight the key worldview assumptions at play, assumptions that continue to run through prominent currents of feminism

[19] De Beauvoir, *The Second Sex*, 761.
[20] De Beauvoir, *The Second Sex*, 761.
[21] De Beauvoir, *The Second Sex*, 766 (emphasis added).

nearly eight decades later. Too often, freedom for women is cast as *freedom from femaleness*. "Autonomy" is envisioned according to male parameters, and women are expected to use invasive chemical and surgical means to conform their bodies to that ideal. Women are not valued simply for *being*; they must prove their value by *doing*. The actions and activities that are marked as laudatory by society are rarely those associated with domesticity and motherhood.

While few feminists now would claim to be self-consciously existentialist, I would argue that Simone de Beauvoir's understanding of freedom and autonomy continue to animate the pro-abortion feminist position. That famous line in *Planned Parenthood v. Casey*, the Supreme Court decision to uphold abortion as a right, has clear existentialist undertones: "At the heart of liberty is the right to define one's own concept of existence, of meaning, of the universe, and of the mystery of human life." There is no sense, in this statement, that there is a *givenness* to the world to which we are accountable, that an unborn human being might exist whether we like it or not, and the fact of that existence might demand a particular ethical response from us. Gone is the ancient view that meaning exists inherently in the world and can be recognized by human beings. Gone is the understanding of a shared human flourishing or *eudaimonia* that is achieved by living in accordance with our nature. Gone, in fact, is the idea of human nature altogether. The only *telos* is an open-ended freedom, an endless journey of self-creation with no particular destination. One's *telos* is to define one's *telos*.

Postmodern Feminism

After the "sex wars" of the 1980s, feminism took a decidedly postmodern turn and has been hurtling in that direction ever since. A key figure at the helm of this shift is philosopher Judith Butler, whose work propelled a move away from *women's studies* toward *gender studies*. Butler's writings have gained canonical prominence in the academy. I'd make the risk-free wager that every gender studies program currently in existence includes Judith Butler's work. It's difficult to overestimate her godlike standing in the field.

I remember seeing Butler speak at the 2008 MLA Convention in Los Angeles. This was during my own postmodern heyday. I was busy dissertating and testing the brutal waters of the academic job market for the first time. As soon as I saw her name on the schedule, I vowed to attend that session, feeling a thrill that I would be able to see Judith Butler with my own eyes, in the flesh.

The large convention room was packed, and I secured a spot near the back. I was surprised at Butler's small stature, a contrast to her legendary status. She sported a boyish haircut, flipped to the side, and a smart leather jacket. As is customary at literary academic conferences, she read steadily and precisely from an essay prepared beforehand. I frantically scribbled notes in a small green notebook, trying to track with the steady flow of ten-dollar words echoing from the podium. I remember thinking to myself as I transcribed: *I have no idea what she is talking about.* This should have given me pause, but it didn't. I just dutifully collected her words, assuming their sagacity was out of my reach, like distant clouds passing overhead, and I would have to meditate carefully on them to discern their meaning. I never for a moment doubted that what she was saying was deeply profound and unassailable. Instead, I doubted myself.

To be fair, Butler is brilliant. She's an intellectual heavyweight, and her prose is like a brick wall; the reader has to butt her head against the words to see a way through. In

1998, Butler infamously won first prize in the "Bad Writing Award" from the journal *Literature and Philosophy* for this sentence:

> The move from a structuralist account in which capital is understood to structure social relations in relatively homologous ways to a view of hegemony in which power relations are subject to repetition, convergence, and rearticulation brought the question of temporality into the thinking of structure, and marked a shift from a form of Althusserian theory that takes structural totalities as theoretical objects to one in which the insights into the contingent possibility of structure inaugurate a renewed conception of hegemony as bound up with the contingent sites and strategies of the rearticulation of power.[22]

I refer to this ignominious honor not to take an easy potshot, but to make a point: one of the dangers of gender and feminist theory is its inscrutability. In my years reading and teaching Butler's writing, I have never seen a student correctly grasp the full implications of her argument. They latch onto those aspects that are intelligible and jibe with their experiences, and on the basis of that minimal confirmation, embrace the rest wholesale. This creates a phenomenon of what I call "trickle-down gender theory": the widespread popular acceptance of ideas that spring from a worldview that most people, particularly most Christians, would reject. Because that worldview is never clearly articulated, it is smuggled aboard unseen.

Many of Butler's foundational assumptions exercise a profound influence in popular culture today, often in

---

[22] "The World's Worst Writing", *The Guardian*, December 24, 1999, https://www.theguardian.com/books/1999/dec/24/news#:~:text=%22The%20move%20from%20a%20structuralist,of%20structure%2C%20and%20marked%20a.

diluted, trickle-down forms. Butler leans into many of the ideas asserted in *The Second Sex*, ascending to new extremes. Butler is heavily influenced by existentialist philosophy, as evidenced by her reference to both de Beauvoir and Jean-Paul Sartre on the first page of her most famous book, *Gender Trouble*. Near the end of *The Second Sex*, de Beauvoir proclaims, "nothing is natural."[23] For Butler, that statement is a foundational premise. *Nothing is natural.*

When de Beauvoir writes that one is not born but becomes a woman, she is driving a wedge between "woman" and "female", arguing that "woman" is a social and cultural fiction that is layered onto the biological reality of femaleness. She writes this in the 1940s, prefiguring the postmodern turn. It didn't take long for a movement centered on the idea of womanhood to begin, bit by bit, dismantling that very category. Since the 1980s, much time and ink has been spent on feminist writing that rejects the stable category of "woman". This is a direct consequence of the postmodern turn, which leads to an interesting conundrum as feminist theory begins enthusiastically sawing off the branch it is sitting on.

In the 1990s, Butler ups the ante, interrogating the concept of "female" as well: "'female' no longer appears to be a stable notion, its meaning is as troubled and unfixed as 'woman'", she writes in *Gender Trouble*.[24] With this move, Butler extends the feminist flight from essentialism into a new frontier. De Beauvoir may have viewed femaleness in negative and even pathological terms, but at least she took it seriously as a "facticity" that grounds and circumscribes the lives of women. Butler, in contrast, does not. This is

[23] De Beauvoir, *The Second Sex*, 761.

[24] Judith Butler, *Gender Trouble: Feminism and the Subversion of Identity* (New York: Routledge, 1990), ix.

because her primary goal as a theorist is to dismantle the normalization of heterosexual relationships—the tendency to see the male and female sexual relationship as normal and natural, which in theory-speak is called *heteronormativity*. The idea that humankind is split into two sexes that are biologically complementary is, for Butler, a social fiction rather than a matter of fact. How does she reach that conclusion, which cuts against both common sense and scientific consensus? In a word: Foucault.

The key to comprehending Judith Butler is to grasp her reliance on the postmodern philosophy of Michel Foucault. I realize, at this point, some of my readers may feel as though I'm showing them an unnecessarily complex series of theoretical nesting dolls—*crack open the Butler doll and inside you find ... Foucault!* In truth, I'm at risk of oversimplifying things, because if Butler's work were a nesting doll, you'd find dozens of little French babies inside: Foucault, yes, and de Beauvoir—and also Derrida, Lacan, Irigaray, Kristeva, Wittig. I will skip the exhaustive genealogy and zero in on Foucault, because he is the man behind the curtain of today's identitarian politics. I would argue that most adherents of the gender paradigm have unwittingly adopted a de facto Foucauldian worldview, inherited, at least in part, through trickle-down Judith Butler.

Let's look at a passage from her book *Undoing Gender*:

> The question of who and what is considered real and true is apparently a question of knowledge. But it is also, as Michel Foucault makes plain, a question of power. Having or bearing "truth" and "reality" is an enormously powerful prerogative within the social world, one way that power dissimulates as ontology.[25]

[25] Judith Butler, *Undoing Gender* (New York: Routledge, 2004), 27.

Power dissimulates as ontology. Ontology refers to the philosophy of being, of what exists. What Butler is saying here is that what we perceive to be "real" is actually a fiction that is created and enforced by institutional power. In the postmodern perspective, truth is suspended in air quotes as ultimately unknowable (or nonexistent). All that remains is power. Knowledge, then, is not a matter of discerning or recognizing what is true, because "truth" itself is a construction of power. Foucault uses the term "knowledge-power" to encapsulate this idea, a term picked up by Butler.

Butler's most famous contribution to gender studies is her concept of gender as a performance. In 1988, she rolls out the theory that what we perceive to be gender is actually an unconscious, socially compelled performance that creates the illusion of an essence.[26] From birth, human beings are categorized by gender and given separate social scripts, so to speak. The continuous enacting of those scripts upholds the illusion that those categories are real, rather than social constructs.

Students tend to latch onto her idea of "gender performativity", because there is a sense in which it is true. Most people have had the experience of playing up their masculinity or femininity in order to conform to sex stereotypes. There is certainly a basic arbitrariness to some of the visible signals of sexual difference in terms of hairstyles and clothing, which vary from culture to culture. There is a sense in which all of us perform, or enact and embody, our sexed identity. What students have a harder time seeing is that Butler is arguing something much more radical. She's saying that sexed identity is *only* a performance, that there is no "real" woman or man underneath the various

---

[26]Judith Butler, "Performative Acts and Gender Constitution: An Essay in Phenomenology and Feminist Theory", *Theatre Journal* 40, no. 4 (1988): 519-31.

cultural expressions. The cultural expressions themselves are merely creating an illusion that men and women exist.

Now, Butler is not denying that biological sex differences exist at all. Rather, she is arguing that any categorization or meaning we ascribe to those differences is a matter of power, not of truth. There's no good reason, in her view, for seeing those differences as any more significant than differences of hair or eye color. The body, for her, exists—but as a blank slate, devoid of its own meaning, upon which social norms are etched.

Butler's theories, like all feminist theory, have a political edge. Recognizing that gender is a fiction allows people to subvert intentionally those norms that create the illusion of reality. "How do drag, butch, femme, transgender, transsexual persons enter the political field?" she asks. "They make us not only question what is real, and what 'must' be, but they also show us how the norms that govern contemporary notions of reality can be questioned and how new modes of reality can become instituted."[27] This is her political project: dismantling the norms of gender and sex in order to dismantle so-called heteronormativity.

To accomplish this, she interrogates *all* norms and mores surrounding sexuality—including the incest taboo. Butler makes the claim that incest is not necessarily traumatic; it's the social stigma that makes it so.[28] Butler evaluates every proposition not by assessing its truth, but by assessing whether it affirms sexual norms. In *Undoing Gender*, she raises the prospect of "replacing the maternal body" with technological innovations that enable artificial reproduction, fully decoupling human reproduction from heterosexual relationships. Butler gives a warning

[27] Butler, *Undoing Gender*, 29.
[28] Butler, *Undoing Gender*, 157.

to feminists who would reject such innovations that their opposition would "*risk naturalizing heterosexual reproduction*".[29] I emphasize that phrase because it pinpoints Butler's extreme social constructionist perspective. The very idea that heterosexual reproduction is natural is, for Butler, a harmful script that must be entirely rewritten.

This postmodern understanding of truth-as-power leads to a postmodern political praxis, in which language is intentionally manipulated to institute these "new modes of reality".[30] That is why there is so much emphasis on policing speech—creating new pronouns and mandating their use, constantly changing the definitions of terms like *gender*, continually proliferating new categories and subcategories of identity and desire. This is a concerted effort to enforce a new social truth-script through an exercise of power.

In the course of writing this book, I came across a claim that Michel Foucault advocated for legalizing pedophilia in France through the removal of age-of-consent laws. This sounded so extreme that I wondered if it was just a conspiracy theory. To my dismay, I discovered it was true. In 1977, Foucault formally petitioned the French government to decriminalize consensual sex with minors.[31] He did not merely propose lowering the age of consent; he proposed abolishing it altogether.[32] That same year, an open letter

---

[29] Butler, *Undoing Gender*, 11.

[30] Butler, *Undoing Gender*, 29.

[31] "Lettre ouverte à la Commission de révision du code pénal pour la révision de certains textes régissant les rapports entre adultes et mineurs", 1977, http://www.dolto.fr/fd-code-penal-crp.html.

[32] Lawrence Kritzman, "Sexual Morality and the Law", in *Michel Foucault— Politics, Philosophy, Culture: Interviews and Other Writings 1977–1984* (New York: Routledge, 1988), 271–85. This is a translated transcription of a 1978 interview in which Foucault discusses his support for the petition, stating that "an age barrier laid down by law does not have much sense". https://www.uib.no/sites/w3.uib.no/files/attachments/foucaultdangerchildsexuality_0.pdf.

in the French newspaper *Le Monde* called for the release of three convicted pedophiles, because "three years [of imprisonment] for kisses and caresses are enough."[33] The letter argues that if thirteen-year-old girls are old enough to be put on the birth control pill, they are old enough to consent to sex with adults. Simone de Beauvoir signed this letter—as did Jean-Paul Sartre, Jean-François Lyotard, Gilles Deleuze, Félix Guattari, and Roland Barthes. All of these figures are superstars in the academy, revered theorists and philosophers. I read all of them in graduate school, unaware that their theoretical assumptions brought them to the conclusion that temporarily sterilizing underage girls so they can have sex with men is perfectly fine.

If your philosophy leads you there, there is something rotten at the root.

Intersectional Feminism

Judith Butler's theories have inarguably shaped the gender paradigm, but those theories morph once they are swept into the capricious winds of popular culture. For example, Butler's early work, particularly her hit concept of performativity, does not align with the transgender narrative of having a gendered essence that is in the wrong body. A trans-identifying man might claim that he is "really" a woman, that his internal sense of gender is more real than his physical sex. This is an essentialist narrative, one that cuts against Butler's denial of gender having any essence at all.

In her later work, Butler adapts. There seems to be a feedback loop; Butler's theories affect culture, and culture

---

[33] *Le Monde*, January 26, 1977, https://www.ipce.info/ipceweb/Library /00aug29b1_from_1977.htm.

in turn influences her subsequent writings. Because her theories are not tethered to reality, to anything stable, she can improvise. By the time *Undoing Gender* is published in 2004, she tempers her language to accommodate transgender politics, and she also expands her rhetoric from a focus on queer identities to include cursory nods to other marginalizing identity factors, like race and disability. This rhetorical shift in Butler's own work reflects a broader shift in feminist and gender theory as a whole, as feminism enters its fourth wave and the concept of "intersectionality" ascends to claim the theory throne.

Intersectionality is a term coined in 1989 by black feminist theorist Kimberlé Crenshaw.[34] In her writing, Crenshaw, a legal scholar, highlighted what she saw as a potential gap in antidiscrimination law. While race and sex are both protected classes, the law does not necessarily recognize unique forms of discrimination that could arise when an individual occupies more than one of those categories. In other words, a black woman could experience a double form of discrimination related to her location at the "intersection" of race and sex, a location that is distinct from that of a black man or a white woman.

There is something straightforwardly true about this insight. There is no monolithic "woman's experience" or "black experience"; other factors, such as class and disability, frame the concrete realities within which individuals live. When used simply as a heuristic or a tool for analysis, the basic idea of intersectionality has the ability to increase

---

[34] Kimberlé Crenshaw, "Demarginalizing the Intersection of Race and Sex: A Black Feminist Critique of Antidiscrimination Doctrine, Feminist Theory and Antiracist Politics", *University of Chicago Legal Forum* (1989). See also her more famous essay "Mapping the Margins: Intersectionality, Identity Politics, and Violence against Women of Color", *Stanford Law Review* 43, no. 6 (July 1991): 1241–99.

our compassion toward other people. Feminist analysis in particular should reflect an awareness of women's multifaceted circumstances. Too often, feminism has revolved around the lives of middle- and upper-class white women, which has been a problem for the movement historically. Second-wave feminism, after all, erupted in response to the bleak depiction of suburban American housewifery in *The Feminine Mystique*. Intersectionality has the potential to add needed complexity to the idea of a diffuse, omnipresent patriarchy that ensures women are always and everywhere disadvantaged in relation to men. Unfortunately, that's not how the concept is typically used in contemporary feminist rhetoric.

I remember biking home recently at the end of a workday. The air was crisp, and I cut through it speedily, feeling my legs churn with strength and vigor. I was eager to be home. I knew that a warm house, a hot meal, and a crew of noisy, healthy children awaited me. My house is close to the local parish, which offers a free evening meal on Fridays. As I neared home, I saw a man walking toward me on the opposite side of the street. Or rather, he was hobbling, his left leg dragging slightly as he swung it forward with great effort. His clothes were ragged, his face weathered, his expression set with a look of grim determination, as if he were walking into a powerful headwind. I assumed he had been at the parish for the free meal, and as I sped by him, two thoughts raced through my head, one on the heels of the other. The first thought: a sudden awareness of how lucky I am to have a healthy body, a stable job, and secure access to housing and food. The second thought: how absurdly reductive and simplistic the concept of "white male privilege" is! How insulting it would be to tell that man that he is somehow, just because of his sex, in a position of power over me, a well-educated, able-bodied, white-collared professor. On one level, my recognition of this was an intersectional insight, because it was based on my perception of the man's class and disability, as well as his sex. Ironically, however, that bludgeon of "white male privilege" is itself a product of intersectional thinking, which has expanded well beyond its role as an analytical tool to become a totalizing ideology, which I will call *intersectionalism*, an ideology that generates divisiveness rather than compassion.

Like the gender paradigm, intersectionalism assumes a postmodern understanding of reality, adapted from the theory of Michel Foucault, the same worldview that underlies Butler's gender theory. Remember, in a Foucauldian understanding of reality, what we assert to be *truth* and *knowledge* is a matter of power. Those who have power define what is real and what can be known. To quote a Butlerism, "to live is to live a life politically, in relation to power."[35] Rather than adding nuance to the idea of an ever-present patriarchy, intersectionalism instead layers on even more pervasive forces of oppression. The villain of "patriarchy" morphs into the archnemesis of "cis white male hetero-patriarchy". The constant spawning of neologisms like "cisgender" is another marker of intersectionalism, which relies on the manipulation of language as a way to reshape what is considered "real".

Intersectionalism erases the dimension of the *universal* as well as the *individual*. We can no longer appeal to a shared human nature or condition that is intrinsic and cross-cultural. Neither can we turn our attention to the individual; we must instead look at people through the lens of identity categories in order to discern whether their perspectives have any value. Human beings are defined or

---

[35] Butler, *Undoing Gender*, 39.

"constituted" by their position on the grid of interlocking forces of oppression. We are not unique individuals; we are Frankensteinian composites, stitched-together hubs of group membership.

These group affiliations are hierarchically ordered and awarded varying degrees of social capital in an attempt to reverse oppressive power dynamics, to recenter the marginalized, to privilege the underprivileged. The attempt simply to reverse power dynamics, however, does nothing to undo an underlying preoccupation with power and domination. Claiming an oppressed identity itself becomes a mode of power. This zero-sum approach leads to a gameable system of endless jockeying for a better position on the oppression pyramid. Like Joseph, with his dreamcoat of many colors, whoever sports the greatest array of marginalized memberships is awarded social dominance over peers.

Notably, among the array of marginalizing forces, economic class tends to receive less emphasis, beyond a cameo appearance in the standard litany of oppressed identities. I suspect that the sidelining of class has something to do with the fact that intersectionalism predominates in well-educated, bourgeoisie spheres, like Ivy League campuses and corporate HR trainings. If economic class were given better real estate on the Intersectional Monopoly board, it would be hard for a tenure-track professor at a world-class institution making a six-figure salary to claim, for example, that she is oppressed because she is a woman or gay or nonwhite—or better yet, all of the above.

The endemic power dynamics of intersectionalism also lead to bizarre in-fighting *within* oppressed categories. For example, the POC category (People of Color), which was standard in academic circles for a while, has now been replaced by BIPOC (black and indigenous people of color), creating an implicit hierarchy of those groups over other minorities, like Asians and Latinos, who are increasingly considered to be "white adjacent". Similarly, transgender identities now trump lesbian and gay identities or even some racial identities, leading to head-spinning proclamations like "cis straight black men are the white people of black people."[36] In heightened intersectional rhetoric such as this, social categorization is too often used as a tool of judgment and censorship, rather than expansive compassion. The dynamics of conflict and domination are not disrupted by intersectionalism, but rather co-opted and redirected.

†

Where does this leave us? What is "the feminist worldview" today? I fully concede that it is difficult, perhaps impossible, to define *the* feminist worldview. However, I do think it is possible to locate prominent theoretical streams that shape and direct contemporary thought, rhetoric, and practice, particularly at the popular level. These streams, taken together, create a de facto worldview, a set of guiding assumptions about reality, the human person, and what true freedom looks like. This implicit worldview is what I am calling the *gender paradigm*.

First and foremost, this paradigm is a godless one. This is taken for granted. We are not created beings; we are products of social forces. Reality, gender, sex—everything, even truth—is socially constructed. A denial of God leads to a denial of nature. By "nature", I do not mean the

---

[36] This specific phrase made a splash on Twitter in 2016. See Damon Young, "Straight Black Men Are the White People of Black People", *The Root*, September 17, 2017, https://www.theroot.com/straight-black-men-are-the-white-people-of-black-people-1814157214.

natural world of plants and animals, but rather the idea of "human nature", the notion that some aspects of human identity are pre-social and intrinsic—influenced by social forces, yes, but not wholly created by them. Because *telos* is connected to *nature*, what we are meant for is connected to who we are. A rejection of God and nature entails a rejection of teleology. Freedom no longer means being free to live in harmony with our nature, to fulfill our inherent potential; freedom is simply the pursuit of unfettered choice, endlessly pushing past limits and norms. This leads to another consequence: the denigration of the body, because *the body itself is a limit*. The concrete reality of the body and sexual difference puts a limit on choice, a limit on self-improvisation, a limit on social construction. The gender paradigm, then, ultimately holds a negative view of embodiment.

My aim in this chapter has been to provide a brief tour of feminism, both its historic arc and present forms, and its relationship to gender theory. The rest of the book will take thematic plunges, adding depth to breadth, with more sustained looks at sex, gender, and embodiment. While the dominant streams I've discussed here all share foundational assumptions, it's important to note that these viewpoints are not always harmonious, but have tensions within and between them. The gender paradigm is not necessarily a coherent worldview, but fraught with internal contradiction. Nonetheless, I think it is not only possible, but *necessary*, to give an account of this framework, in order to understand how this framework differs from a Christian one. Only from that foundation—from a solid understanding of competing worldviews—is it possible for Christians to mine feminist thought and praxis for hidden gems and to partner with secular feminists toward shared goals.

Control

In 1930, a Danish artist named Einar Wegener underwent the first of four surgeries in an attempt to change his sex. Wegener had been regularly dressing and presenting as a woman for several years, occasionally going by the name "Lili". Wegener was one of the first people to have what is now called sex reassignment surgery (or "gender confirmation" surgery). In the 1930s, this was a novel phenomenon, the procedures entirely experimental.

Wegener first heard of the tantalizing prospect of changing his sex from the German Institute for Sex Research, run by Magnus Hirschfeld, a German physician who coined the term "transsexual". Wegener was transfixed by the desire to become a "complete woman", which included the ability to carry and bear children.[1] For him, becoming a woman was not simply a matter of "passing" or appearing to be a woman; he wanted a true sex change, the ability to adopt the procreative potentiality of a female. He wanted to be completely reborn. His story reads almost like a retelling of Eve's creation: a man falling into the sleep of nonbeing, so a new female creation can emerge. However, in this case, there is no divine force at work, only the will of man and the untried power of his *technê*.

As part of his transformation, Wegener parted ways from his wife, Gerda, and legally changed his name to Lili

[1] Niels Hoyer, ed., *Man into Woman: An Authentic Record of a Change of Sex* (New York: E.P. Dutton & Co., 1933), https://www.lilielbe.org/narrative/editions/A1.html.

Elbe, christening his new self after the river that winds its way through Europe. He also took a male lover, hoping to one day bear this man's children, once *he* had fully emerged from the chrysalis as *she*.

Wegener entrusted himself to Hirschfeld's care, enduring four invasive surgeries in less than two years. First, his testicles were removed, followed by an ovarian transplant in his abdomen. The third procedure removed his penis and scrotum, and the final surgery involved both a uterine transplant and the construction of a vaginal canal. Tragically and predictably, his immune system rejected the alien uterus, and Elbe died in 1931, three months after his last surgery. He was forty-eight years old.

The story of Einar Wegener was not widely known until told in the 2015 film *The Danish Girl*. This is not true of Christine Jorgensen, born George William Jorgensen, an American man who during the mid-twentieth century became the first trans celebrity, appearing on magazine covers and touring the nation to advocate for transgender people, then known as transsexuals. Jorgensen's medical transition, which began in 1952, differed from Wegener's in two key ways. By the 1950s, endocrinologists had developed the ability to synthesize and manipulate sex hormones, a technological innovation that also facilitated the development of the first hormonal contraceptive pill. Jorgensen began his transition by taking cross-sex hormones—the name "Christine" is an homage to Jorgensen's endocrinologist, Christian Hamburger—and then having his testicles and penis removed, as well as undergoing a subsequent vaginoplasty. This is the second key difference: Jorgensen's transition left him permanently sterilized, yet he made no attempt to pursue the fertile potentiality of a female. He did not share Wegener's understanding of what it meant to become a "complete woman".

Wegener and Jorgensen are different people, of course, with distinct desires and motivations. Moreover, transplanting foreign organs into a body is much riskier than removing native organs, to be sure—a risk that proved fatal for Wegener. Yet I think there is another layer to the story that is worth telling, a broader shift in the cultural understanding of what it means to be a woman. Jorgensen did not apparently think that he needed the potential to bear children in order to become a "real" woman. More tellingly, neither did society. In 1930, the pursuit of womanhood involved adopting the female procreative role. By the 1950s, womanhood had become simply a matter of reshaping one's appearance. What is behind this conceptual shift? What unfolded in those intervening decades? The widespread normalization of contraception.

No Gods, No Masters

The early feminist suffragettes were not proponents of contraception. While they did advocate for "voluntary motherhood", the mechanism was periodic abstinence: women's right to say no to sex, even within the context of marriage. This put the onus of family planning on both the man and the woman; women would be given legal protection against marital rape, and men would be asked to curb their desires for the sake of regulating births. In fact, many suffragettes saw contraception as something that would benefit *men* rather than women, allowing men more sexual license once freed from the prospect of fathering a child.

These first-wave feminists located the source of female oppression in external social forces, particularly the legal system. But one influential activist, Margaret Sanger, decided the suffragettes were misguided, focused on the wrong things. The changes they fought for would not make women free, she concluded, because women are not ultimately oppressed by society or men or bad laws. Women are oppressed by their own bodies:

> [Woman] claimed the right of suffrage and legislative regulation of her working hours, and asked that her property rights be equal to those of the man. None of these demands, however, affected directly the most vital factors of her existence... She had chained herself to her place in society and the family through the maternal functions of her nature, and only chains thus strong could have bound her to her lot as a brood animal for the masculine civilizations of the world ... woman has, through her reproductive ability, founded and perpetuated the tyrannies of the Earth. Whether it was the tyranny of a monarchy, an oligarchy or a republic, the one indispensable factor of its existence was, as it is now, hordes of human beings— human beings so plentiful as to be cheap, and so cheap that ignorance was their natural lot. Upon the rock of an unenlightened, submissive maternity have these been founded; upon the product of such a maternity have they flourished.[2]

This is an excerpt from Sanger's book *Woman and the New Race*, published in 1920. The chapter title is telling: "Woman's Error and Her Debt". The error? Having too many babies, which has led to all the world's problems. The debt? She must remake the world by "freeing herself from the chains of her own reproductivity." Sanger does not only think women are oppressed by their biology; she also charges them with perpetuating evil. Tyranny is no

[2] Margaret Sanger, *Woman and the New Race* (New York: Brentano, 1920), accessed via Project Gutenberg, http://www.gutenberg.org/cache/epub/8660 /pg8660.html.

longer the fault of the tyrant; it is the mothers we should blame. Female fecundity thus becomes the scapegoat for woman's oppression, as well as everything wrong with the world.

The birth control movement in America, founded by Sanger, was resoundingly eugenicist. One can see this clearly from Sanger's own writings. She is not ultimately concerned with the well-being of individual women, although that is part of her project to be sure. Her ultimate goal is to purge the earth of unfit human beings, those "meaningless, aimless lives which cram this world of ours ... yet who have done absolutely nothing to advance the race one iota. Their lives are hopeless repetitions.... Such human weeds clog up the path, drain up the energies and the resources of this little earth."[3] Sanger's eugenicist views are thankfully offensive to most modern ears, but her view of birth control as a global panacea has become unquestionable. However, in her day, the early twentieth century, the reverse was true: eugenicist views were widely accepted, particularly among the elite, whereas the question of birth control was still controversial.

Sanger began her activist work in 1914 by publishing a newsletter promoting contraception with the slogan "no gods, no masters", a slogan that has been adopted by today's antifascist anarchists. In 1916, she opened the first birth control clinic in the United States, and in the early 1920s, she founded the first iteration of what would become Planned Parenthood, the American Birth Control League. By 1929, Sanger was actively lobbying the U.S. government to legalize contraception. Thanks to Sanger's efforts, contraception

[3] Alexander Sanger, "Eugenics, Race, and Margaret Sanger Revisited: Reproductive Freedom for All?", *Hypatia* 22, no. 2 (2007): 215.

was readily available even if still prohibited. Sanger had successfully popularized the term "birth control", which had become ensconced in American vernacular. In the early 1950s, Sanger collaborated with Katharine McCormick and Gregory Pincus to develop the first hormonal contraceptive pill, and it was approved by the FDA in 1957.

Reading Sanger's writings is a bit of an emotional roller coaster. On the one hand, her hyperbolic rhetoric exposes very real social problems. She is right to be enraged at the thousands of women who felt compelled to seek illegal abortions. She is right to critique a society that puts women in that horrific position. I share her distaste for war, for tyranny, for oppression. Yet her analysis of these problems is repellant. She blames women's bodies and dehumanizes human beings who do not, in her mind, sufficiently "advance the race". This perspective is in lockstep with the triumphalist progressive narrative of her day. The way into the Crystal Palace utopia of the future is paved by advances in science, technology, and the continual conquest of nature.

All the Axial religions, including ancient philosophical schools such as Stoicism and Confucianism, affirm the necessity of regulating desire in order to live in accord with nature—both with our bodies and with the whole of creation. Enlightenment progressivism, in contrast, objectifies nature as a force to be controlled. *Control*. That is the cornerstone of Sanger's ideology.[4] This is not control over our passions and destructive desires, an ideal Sanger calls "an absurdity".[5] This is control over biology, over nature

---

[4] I'm drawing here on the work of theologian Angela Franks, who rightly characterizes Sanger as professing an ideology of control. See Angela Franks, "A Life of Passion: Progressive Eugenics and Planned Parenthood", *Public Discourse*, January 4, 2021, https://www.thepublicdiscourse.com/2012/01/4445/.

[5] Sanger, *Woman and the New Race*, chap. 4.

herself. Sanger's vision of progress is an inversion of ancient wisdom. Rather than curbing our will to live in harmony with nature, we contort nature to unleash our will.

Simone de Beauvoir's *The Second Sex*, written in 1949, echoes many of Sanger's views, drawing them into a more sophisticated existentialist framework. Like Sanger, de Beauvoir sees women as enslaved by their biology. Like Sanger, de Beauvoir claims that true freedom can only be found in a socialist utopia that enables women to control their bodies with contraception and abortion. Both women implicitly sculpt their vision of freedom according to the male ideal. Women can only find true freedom by making themselves as much like men as possible. De Beauvoir's direct influence on second-wave architect Betty Friedan helps forge an unshakeable alliance between the ideology of control and the feminist movement.

In the span of a few decades, Margaret Sanger brought about a revolution, a shocking reversal, in cultural mores and sentiments. When Sanger began her work advocating for birth control as humankind's savior, she was seen as a radical. Her views on birth control were at odds with the society of her day, even with most feminists. By the end of her life, those views had become standard, even respectable, in society at large, and wholly embraced by feminists in the second wave. From the 1960s onward, feminists have followed in the footsteps of Sanger and de Beauvoir, locating women's oppression in their biology and advocating for a vision of "health" that pathologizes female fertility.

Pathologizing Femaleness

Sanger's cultural coup was successful because she was able to get the doctors on her side. Birth control was rebranded as a matter of "reproductive health", an association that has only strengthened over time. Think of the common shorthand for hormonal contraception: "the pill"—no further details required, as if there is a singular magic remedy that women need to guarantee health and freedom.

The "disorder" requiring medical intervention? The normal function of a woman's body. Healthy female bodies, after all, are fertile. There is a troubling assumption at work here, underlying the designation of the pill as the fulcrum of women's health: women, to be "healthy" and "free", must function, biologically speaking, as much like men as possible. Sanger's writings make explicit her view that female fecundity is not natural and good, but *pathological*—a dangerous disease that needs to be treated and controlled. This view has become entrenched in our culture. Access to birth control and abortion are all but synonymous with "reproductive health", a clever term that sounds pro-woman but actually pathologizes natural biological realities that are unique to women, namely fertility, pregnancy, and childbirth.

The term "health" has dual etymological roots: a word in Old English that means "wholeness" and a word in Old Norse that means "holy or sacred". Health is wholeness, when the order and harmony of the body is in good working condition, when all is functioning as it is supposed to. The work of healing, then, is *a restoration of wholeness*. There is something sacred about that very harmony and order, about restoring the natural processes of the body. A Christian vision of women's health is one that sees female physiology in terms of wholeness rather than pathology and works with, not against, the natural order of the female body.

This perspective is squarely at odds with both mainstream feminism and the medical establishment, which have embraced the paradigm of pathology. The most widely used and prescribed methods of birth control, such as synthetic hormones and/or an intrauterine device (IUD), work by disrupting the normal functions of a woman's reproductive system, intentionally making it *malfunction*, in order to prevent pregnancy. Unsurprisingly, the disruption of one organ system can disrupt the equilibrium of the entire organism, which leads to increased risks for serious disease.

According to the National Cancer Institute, a metanalysis of 54 studies concluded that women who are using oral contraceptives have a 24% increased risk of breast cancer.[6] A 2017 Danish study indicated that women with current or recent use of oral contraceptives had a 20% higher risk of breast cancer overall, and depending on the specific kind of pill, a risk as high as 60%.[7] Moreover, the risk of breast cancer increased the longer oral contraceptives were used. The Danish study is particularly noteworthy, because it focuses on recent formulations of the birth control pill, rather than older versions with higher doses of synthetic hormones. Use of oral contraceptives has also been shown to increase the risk of cervical cancer—the longer the usage, the higher the risks. With five or fewer years of use, the elevated risk is 10%. With five to nine years of use, this risk increases to 60% and doubles again with ten or more years of use.[8]

On the other hand, use of oral contraceptives actually *lowers* the risk of endometrial and ovarian cancers by at least

[6] See "Oral Contraceptives and Cancer Risk", National Cancer Institute, last updated February 22, 2018, https://www.cancer.gov/about-cancer/causes -prevention/risk/hormones/oral-contraceptives-fact-sheet#what-is-known -about-the-relationship-between-oral-contraceptive-use-and-cancer.

[7] L. S. Mørch et al., "Contemporary Hormonal Contraception and the Risk of Breast Cancer", *New England Journal of Medicine* 377, no. 23 (2017): 2228–39, https://doi.org/10.1056/NEJMoa1700732.

[8] J. S. Smith et al., "Cervical Cancer and Use of Hormonal Contraceptives: A Systematic Review", *Lancet* 361, no. 9364 (2003): 1159–67, https://doi.org /10.1016/s0140-6736(03)12949-2.

30%.[9] Do these relative risks then cancel each other out? That's one way of reading it. The protective value against ovarian cancer is due to a reduction in the overall ovulations and menstrual periods a woman experiences in her lifetime. This reduction can be *naturally* accomplished by the processes of pregnancy, childbirth, and lactation, the very processes that the pill tries to suppress. Pregnancy and breastfeeding, in fact, not only lower the risk of ovarian and endometrial cancers; they also lower the risk of breast cancer. A history of breastfeeding, moreover, increases the survival rates of women who do develop breast cancer. Avoiding oral contraceptives and experiencing the normal physiological processes of pregnancy, birth, and lactation, then, provide the optimal combination: a lowered risk of cancers across the board.

Hormonal birth control can also wreak havoc on a woman's mental and emotional well-being. The pill increases the risk of developing depression, according to a 2016 study of over a million women living in Denmark.[10] The risk was actually higher with progesterone-only forms of contraception, including the IUD: "That the IUD was particularly associated with depression in all age groups is especially significant, because traditionally, physicians have been taught that the IUD only acts locally and has no effects on the rest of the body. Clearly, this is not accurate."[11] The risk of depression was most elevated

[9] K. A. Michels et al., "Modification of the Associations between Duration of Oral Contraceptive Use and Ovarian, Endometrial, Breast, and Colorectal Cancers", *JAMA Oncology* 4, no. 4 (2018): 516–21.

[10] C. W. Skovlund, L. S. Mørch, and L. V. Kessing, "Association of Hormonal Contraception with Depression", *JAMA Psychiatry* 73, no. 11 (2016): 1154–62.

[11] Monique Tello, "Can Hormonal Birth Control Trigger Depression?", *Harvard Health Blog*, October 1, 2019, https://www.health.harvard.edu/blog/can-hormonal-birth-control-trigger-depression-2016101710514.

for adolescent girls, a demographic whose mental health is currently in serious crisis.

These increased risks for debilitating conditions, like cancer and depression as well as blood clots and stroke, are accompanied by other common side effects: migraines, weight gain, decreased libido, mood swings. No wonder many women abandon their chosen method of artificial birth control after several years. According to the Contraception CHOICE project, a cohort study of 10,000 women aged 14–45, "69% of the women who had chosen oral contraceptives, injection, the vaginal ring or the skin patch had given up on them after three years."[12] Even the IUD, which seems better in comparison, has dropout rates of close to 50% within five years, largely due to side effects such as bleeding or pain, or because the IUD perforated the uterus and was expelled from the body. These statistics clearly indicate women's widespread dissatisfaction with available birth control methods, belying the triumphalist line that contraception is the golden key to women's reproductive health and freedom.

There's another layer to this exposé: the go-to medical practice of disrupting a woman's hormonal ecosystem to suppress ovulation—or address any reproductive malady— is not based on good science. In 2019, *Scientific American* issued a special report on women's reproductive health. As expected, the report takes pains to affirm the standard platitude—contraception makes women free!—but only as a disclaimer. The bulk of the report offers surprising critiques of the medical establishment's enthusiastic attitude toward birth control and discusses how that enthusiasm can be an impediment to women's health. The report accuses

---

[12] Maya Dusenbery, "Why Women—and Men—Need Better Birth Control", *Scientific American*, May 2019, 44.

clinicians of "wield[ing] synthetic hormones like a hammer, liberally prescribing the birth control pill for all kinds of pain."[13] This blundering enthusiasm can actually obscure the nature of an underlying disease, such as endometriosis, which, on average, takes eight years to be diagnosed.[14]

The first article in the report, "What is the Point of a Period?", highlights the dearth of knowledge among doctors about the natural functions of the female reproductive system and cycles, particularly the menstrual cycle. In the rush to bring so-called "reproductive freedom" to women, those pioneers of the birth control pill—Margaret Sanger, Gregory Pincus, John Rock—"appear to have ignored the implications of shutting down a woman's natural cycle. [They] figured out how to supplant periods long before they began trying to understand why they work the way they do."[15] To most in the medical establishment, the pill is seen and prescribed as a magic bullet for all kinds of physical issues and irregularities. Elizabeth Kissling, professor of women's and gender studies at Eastern Washington University, disagrees: "The pill isn't a treatment for [menstrual irregularities], it's a way of refusing to treat them.... Doctors are so quick to prescribe the drug to teenagers reporting bad cramps without investigating to see if there is an underlying cause." Like Kissling, I am concerned with the trend of prescribing the pill for long-term period suppression without adequate knowledge about the potential ramifications. This practice, Kissling says, is "the largest uncontrolled medical experiment on women in history."[16]

---

[13] Clara Moskowitz and Jen Schwartz, "Fertile Ground", *Scientific American*, May 2019, 31.

[14] Moskowitz and Schwartz, "Fertile Ground".

[15] Virginia Sole-Smith, "The Point of a Period", *Scientific American*, May 2019, 35–36.

[16] Sole-Smith, "The Point of a Period", 39–40.

What is the alternative? Sanger's work, however flawed it might be, did recognize that poor and working-class women were often placed in desperate circumstances. While she put the blame primarily on female fertility, I would shift it elsewhere: to the lack of social support for these women, the cultural expectation that women should always be sexually available to men, and limited awareness about a woman's fertility cycle. Women in Sanger's time did not have access to the kinds of tools and knowledge available today—knowledge that, unfortunately, has not yet become mainstream in the medical profession or among women themselves. Women and girls are routinely prescribed medication that suppresses their natural cycles but are rarely educated about how to better understand and "read" those cycles. This doesn't have to be the case.

According to a 2012 study, the top three features women desire in a birth control method are (1) effectiveness, (2) lack of side effects, and (3) affordability.[17] The study concludes that "that combination does not exist." In fact, it does, in natural forms of birth control, known as Fertility Awareness Methods (FAMs) or, in Catholic circles, Natural Family Planning (NFP). According to the *Scientific American* report, FAMs are one of the only birth control methods "whose popularity is on the rise".[18]

As the name indicates, FAMs work by training women to track their own cyclical fertility. There are a number of different methods that rely on various combinations of fertility indicators, such as basal body temperature, cervical mucus, and tracking hormones such as estrogen, progesterone, and the luteinizing hormone that triggers ovulation. FAMs have no physiological side effects, because they

[17] Dusenbery, "Better Birth Control", 44.
[18] Dusenbery, "Better Birth Control", 47.

do not seek to disrupt a woman's reproductive system; instead, they attune women to their bodies, so women can make more informed sexual choices. FAMs are also more generally affordable, depending on how technologically advanced one chooses to be, requiring no ongoing prescriptions or medical procedures. They can also be very effective, as affirmed by multiple peer-reviewed studies.[19] The conclusions of these studies show that FAMs, when used properly, are just as or *more* effective than artificial methods of birth control.

FAMs do require, as the name suggests, a heightened and active *awareness* of bodily processes on the part of women. This is not a passive form of birth control, like popping a pill once a day or inserting a piece of metal in the womb. I do not see this as a bad thing. The more aware a woman is of her normal cyclical pattern, the sooner she will notice if something is amiss, which can indicate the presence of a condition that *actually* requires medical attention (unlike, say, simply being female). To be effective as a method of birth control, FAMs do require behavioral changes: in order to avoid pregnancy, a couple must practice periodic abstinence or use a barrier method during the woman's fertile window. The Catholic approach, Natural Family Planning, uses periodic abstinence, which requires active commitment and participation on the part of the man as well as the woman. In NFP, the demands of the method

[19] Here are just two examples. A 2008 study on the Marquette Method of NFP found a correct-use effectiveness rate of 99.4%. See Richard Fehring et al., "Efficacy of the Marquette Method of Natural Family Planning", *The American Journal of Maternal/Child Nursing* 33, no. 6 (2008): 348–54. More recently, a March 2019 study on the effectiveness of the *Dot* fertility awareness app found a perfect-use failure of 1% and a typical-use failure of 5%. See Victoria Jennings et al., "Perfect- and Typical-Use Effectiveness of the Dot Fertility App over 13 Cycles: Results from a Prospective Contraceptive Effectiveness Trial", *The European Journal of Contraception & Reproductive Health Care* 24, no. 2 (2019): 148–53.

rest on the couple, testing their self-restraint and willingness to sacrifice for one another. The responsibility of fertility is not borne by the woman alone.

The key distinction between synthetic methods of birth control and FAMs is this: One seeks to prevent pregnancy by altering a woman's physiology so that it malfunctions and fails to do what it is designed to do. The other can be used either to avoid or achieve pregnancy through a deeper understanding of a woman's physiology, which allows a woman to adapt her behavior in harmony with her physiology. In brief: one works by changing the normal functions of a woman's body; one works by empowering her with greater knowledge of her body.

Despite the continual rhetoric about women's freedom, control, and agency, there seems to be a strong reluctance among doctors to rely *more* on women's agency when it comes to planning pregnancies. Personally, I have never heard FAMs suggested as viable birth control options by a medical professional. When I became interested in natural birth control, I learned about it by talking to other women and doing my own independent research. Any conversations I have had with doctors about my choice to use FAMs invariably result in pressure to switch to the pill or an IUD. Doctors have a marked preference to alter a woman's reproductive system medically, rather than trusting her to read her own fertility and, armed with that knowledge, make behavioral choices to either achieve or avoid pregnancy.

I remember one particular conversation just hours after the birth of my third child. A doctor came into my hospital room to offer a hearty congratulations—before immediately pivoting to ask about my plans for birth control. The implicit and conflicting message seemed to be: "Congratulations on the birth of this beautiful baby! How thrilled you must be! Now: What can we do to make sure *this never happens again*?" She was not happy when I told her that I would be using FAMs, responding with gentle pressure to leave the hospital with a prescription for hormonal birth control.

I dread these postpartum interactions, the doctor's predictable directive to consume synthetic hormones even before my cycles resume. Too often, when I discuss FAMs with physicians, I am met with skepticism and disapproval, as if I'm practicing the archaic rhythm method rather than using scientifically sophisticated and precise techniques to map my unique cyclical pattern. I can tell it makes them nervous—my unwillingness to suppress my fertility, and my refusal to rely on medical interventions rather than my own agency and bodily knowledge.

The current medical paradigm, lauded by most feminists, is a paradigm that pathologizes female fertility, viewing a woman's potential for pregnancy as an adverse condition to be medically managed. This medical management disrupts the wholeness of a woman's body rather than restoring it, and in this way is not in accord with the basic definition of health. A Catholic vision of women's health and family planning, in contrast, would educate medical practitioners and women themselves in methods of fertility awareness, methods that work in harmony with a woman's body rather than against it. This vision, in contrast, provides a fertility-positive approach to women's health, an approach that does not see a woman's body as a threat to her freedom and happiness but rather as something *good*, worthy of deeper understanding and respect.

At Odds with Reality

The endemic use of hormonal birth control might not be good for women's health, but is it good for society?

According to Sanger, women must take the blame and responsibility for social ills upon themselves, becoming salvific martyrs for the good of all. While she does believe that birth control will lead to women's emancipation, she seems more focused on the broader eugenic utopia she assumes birth control will create.

Unfortunately, Sanger is wrong on both fronts: contraception is not good for women, and it is not good for society. We now live in a state of perpetual dissonance. Our shared cultural imagination, as well as the norms and expectations shaped by that understanding, is at odds with reality. We now think of sex as a *recreational*, rather than *procreational*, activity. The connection between sex and the possibility of new life has been severed. We think of women, and women think of themselves, as naturally sterile beings. Pregnancy is often seen as a sexual mishap, a case of sex-gone-wrong, rather than the very outcome that sexual intercourse is designed to bring about. The procreational potential of sex is viewed as a switch that can be flipped, if desired, but whose default setting is "off".

There are numerous consequences of assumed female sterility. One is that the rate of abortions actually *increases*. Sanger hoped that birth control would eradicate abortion and infanticide. She envisioned that in her contraceptive utopia, "there will be no killing of babies in the womb by abortion."[20] The opposite has turned out to be the case. Sanger's own legacy organization, Planned Parenthood, currently performs around 350,000 abortions per year. Once the birth control pill was legalized in America, abortion rates skyrocketed. In 1965, the year that birth control was legalized, the abortion rate was 794. Just five

---

[20] Sanger, *Woman and the New Race*, chap. 18.

years later, that number jumped to 193,491. Within a single decade, 1,034,200 abortions were performed annually in the United States. From fewer to one thousand to over one million: that is an increase of 130,152% in ten years. Even if we assume that abortion rates in 1960 were underreported, it remains undeniable that abortions drastically increased once contraception was widely used.[21]

This increase of abortions upon the legalization of birth control is counterintuitive. I once assumed, like most people, that contraception is the best way to decrease abortions. From one angle, this is partly accurate. When a society first becomes contraceptive, abortion radically increases, as shown with the example of the United States above. In the case of the Soviet Union, however, increasing the availability of contraception *reduced* their sky-high abortion rate, which, in 1988, outpaced live births.[22] This is because at the time the USSR became a contraceptive society, the default method of birth control was abortion. Once an alternate birth control method was introduced, abortion rates came down.

In the United States, however, abortion has functioned as a back-up, a secondary form of birth control when contraception fails. The most accurate way to characterize the dynamic between contraception and abortion, then, is this: when a society normalizes contraception, the rate of abortions will drastically increase. However, in an

---

[21] This data is from the website Historical Abortion Statistics, which draws from a number of sources, including the CDC and the Guttmacher Institute, which was once an affiliate of Planned Parenthood. I cross-checked this data with the CDC and found it to be accurate. See Wm. Robert Johnson, "Historical Abortion Statistics, United States", last modified January 14, 2020, http://www.johnstonsarchive.net/policy/abortion/ab-unitedstates.html.

[22] A. A. Popov, "Family Planning in the USSR. Sky-High Abortion Rates Reflect Dire Lack of Choice", *Entre Nous* 16 (1990): 5–7, PMID 12222340.

already-contraceptive society, use of contraception can keep the abortion rate steady or even lower it slightly. In the United States, for example, the abortion rate peaked in 1990 at 1,608,600, at which point it began to level off, dipping to a current rate of around 850,000 abortions per year. This is still, however, an astronomical jump (106,953%) from the 1965, pre-pill rates. Overall, then, the normalization of contraception—the *default expectation of female sterilization*—vastly increases abortions.

Why is this? Contraception makes a promise that it can't always deliver. The promise: a fertile woman can have sex without getting pregnant. The reality: all birth control methods have failure rates, and when a method fails, our shared fantasy of sterilized sex skids into reality. A woman who finds herself in this position, feeling betrayed by a functioning body, will often seek an abortion. This is the back-up factor: when contraception fails to make good on its promise, abortion fills the gap.

There's another layer of complexity here, and that is the shift in women's self-perception. When I participated in that week-long seminar with philosopher Luce Irigaray, I was joined by ten other Ph.D. students from all over the world. We came from a variety of disciplines, and we each took a turn presenting our doctoral research, followed by feedback from and discussion with Irigaray and the group. The work of one particular researcher has stuck with me. She was a practicing British physician who wanted to understand why so many of her patients were ending up pregnant. These women were on birth control, which the doctor herself had prescribed, and many of them were already mothers, presumably well aware of the realities of pregnancy. Yet again and again, these women turned up in her office with unplanned pregnancies. The researcher had determined that her patients seemed to have "magical thinking" about contraception, but she didn't yet understand why.

I was in my mid-twenties at the time, married and somewhat reluctantly on hormonal birth control. I say reluctantly because, on the one hand, I believed that in order to pursue an academic career, I needed to keep childbearing at bay for the indefinite future. On the other hand, I was also aware that birth control made me irritable, flattened my libido, and came with an increased risk of breast cancer, which runs in my family. When I took this researcher's assessment survey, the results indicated that I, too, was prone to this "magical thinking". I remember our seminar session: a circle of nascent feminist academics, puzzling and speculating about why women on birth control kept getting pregnant. We spun our theorizing wheels, completely oblivious to the most obvious cause: the birth control itself.

Years later, after becoming Catholic and permitting myself to question the supposed benefits of my many years on the pill, I was able to identify what I call the contraceptive paradox: *one effect of using contraception is a reduced awareness of one's "need" for contraception*. In other words, the use of passive birth control methods—those that work on a woman's physiology without her conscious awareness—alter a woman's sense of herself as a fertile being, cultivating instead a consciousness of assumed sterility. This altered consciousness can influence women's choices and actions. For example, if I think of myself as sterile, I might be more likely to engage in casual, riskier sexual behavior, uninhibited by the prospect of long-term consequences. I am also perhaps more likely to forget to take the pill altogether, which I certainly did, numerous times. This reduced awareness of one's capacity for pregnancy can actually increase user failure rates, contributing to the

surprisingly high rate of unplanned pregnancies in the
United States, a rate that persists despite the widespread
use of contraception.[23]

Consumer Sex

Through normalizing contraception, we have erased fertility from our consciousness. This has reshaped—how could
it not?—our shared understanding of the purpose of sex,
which in turn has altered our behavior. No longer is there
an expectation of sexual restraint for some higher good. By
restraint, I'm not gesturing toward a Victorian flight from
the body and sexuality; I'm pointing back even further, to the
ancient philosophers, who all recognized that happiness
lies in the self-balancing work of virtue—cultivated habits
that liberate us from being pawns of our appetites.

As I stand here typing out these thoughts, an image
springs to mind, plucked from a banal archive of recent
memories. I'm on a plane that has just landed, queuing
up in the aisle with all the other passengers. Just in front
of me is a gray-haired man, likely in his sixties, booting
up his cell phone like everyone else. Instead of jumping
to text or email, he opens a dating app. I use the word
"dating", but of course that's a euphemism. He's scrolling
for sex. Women's faces flash across his phone screen; he
swipes most of them away with barely a glance, unbeliev-
ably quickly. I'm peering shamelessly over his shoulder,
unnoticed, and so I see them too: woman after woman,
face after face, some smiling brightly, others tentatively,

[23] Currently, almost half of all pregnancies in the United States are unintended. See "Unintended Pregnancy in the United States", Guttmacher Institute, last visited October 5, 2021, https://www.guttmacher.org/fact-sheet
/unintended-pregnancy-united-states#.

hopefully, some attempting gestures of seduction with lip-pouts and glimpses of skin. He pauses only on the faces that are young, half his age, pressing a button with his thumb to file those women away for later. I think about each woman as her face flicks by. I think about her desire for love, for companionship, to be seen, to be known, to be looked upon with adoration and respect. What woman—what human?—doesn't want these things? We are made for love. That is always what we seek. As I watch this man file through dozens of faces, I feel a slow eruption of rage and disgust in my belly that reaches up into my throat. He is not seeing these women as persons. He is assessing them hastily as potential outlets for his appetites, like scouring a drive-through menu for that burger that will hit the spot.

His gestures are callous, yes, but also frantic, compulsive. We're not even off the plane, after all, and he's already trolling for prey, like a shark circling endlessly, unable to stop moving. He is not in control; he is *being* controlled. Just as his lust obscures the personhood of the faces on his screen, so it also diminishes his own humanity. In making objects of these women, he has made an animal of himself.

This is what sex becomes—what *we* become—when sex is cut off from life. Pope Paul VI predicted this in 1968, in his encyclical *Humanae vitae*. This letter, which defied popular opinion even then, was the Catholic Church's definitive response to the question of whether she should follow other Christian groups in embracing contraception. The Church said no. As part of his response, Paul VI made several predictions that now ring as prophetic. One of them was this:

> Another effect that gives cause for alarm is that a man who grows accustomed to the use of contraceptive methods may forget the reverence due to a woman, and,

disregarding her physical and emotional equilibrium, reduce her to being a mere instrument for the satisfaction of his own desires, no longer considering her as his partner whom he should surround with care and affection.[24]

When I read this paragraph, I think of that man on the plane, the millions like him, and the parade of discarded faces on their screens. We don't need to conjure a false image of an idealized past to recognize that there is something rotten in our culture. It's not as if the sexual exploitation of women was invented in 1965. This is an ancient evil. But the unmooring of sex from life has cheapened it and cheapened us, fueling a consumerist sexual paradigm that trumpets liberation while enslaving us.

Within the consumer-sex paradigm, a new view of the human person emerges, as innate dignity and embodied personhood recede and disappear into the background. This view is an *instrumentalist* view, wherein the person is seen as a tool, an instrument, a means to someone else's self-centered ends. When we speak of the sexual objectification of women, we are referencing this view: a person who is made into an object for use.

The only guiding moral principle in this paradigm is consent. You, a free agent, can do anything you want, as long as it does not compromise the free agency of another. Let me be clear: *consent is crucial.* An emphasis on the importance of consent is perhaps the one good feature of this paradigm. Catholic tradition shares this emphasis on consent; the very definition of a valid marriage depends upon the free choice of each party, to cite just one example. The problem is not that consent is a primary value in this view;

[24] Paul VI, encyclical letter *Humanae vitae* (On Human Life) (July 25, 1968), no. 17.

the problem is that it's the *only* value. Consent should be the starting point rather than the end of the discussion about sexual morality. It is not enough to say that the best we can expect from sex, morally speaking, is that it's *not rape*.

Consent is a precarious and hollow platform on which to build an entire sexual ethics. It does nothing to guard against self-destruction and little to guard against choices that are subtly, even unintentionally, coerced. A woman sells sex to support a drug addiction. Is she freely choosing that profession? Is it empowering her? A porn star who suffered sexual abuse as a child is now choosing to reenact her own exploitation for money. Is this good? How often, after all, are our choices entirely "free"? Only an ethics rooted in the *objective* value of embodied human personhood can draw clear boundaries against sexual abuse and exploitation.

One consequence of the Me Too movement, arguably, has been to reveal the fault lines in the consumerist paradigm, the poverty of a sexual morality that is based purely in consent. This movement has made clear that someone can be misused and harmed by sex that is technically consensual. The era of sexual liberation is not as liberating for women as advertised.

I once made this argument about treating someone as an *end* rather than a *means* in an undergraduate seminar, and my feminist students who were pro-prostitution rejected it immediately. "What about a restaurant server?" they objected. "Aren't you using someone as a means to an end when you pay her to bring you a burger?" The difference, I told them, is that when it comes to prostitution and sexual exploitation, *the person is the burger*. What is being consumed and commodified is not food, but the sex worker's own body, her very self. From a Christian anthropological perspective, sex is not just a bodily activity, but a union of whole persons. This makes the "work" of sex unique, distinct from other kinds of physical labor.

My students were reasoning from a dualist variant of the instrumentalist view, a view that separates the self from the body, making it possible to objectify the body while preserving a phantom of personhood rooted only in the will. This is a riff on the old Cartesian dualism, "I think, therefore I am." Instead of distilling selfhood to rationality, this new mode features the autonomous, desiring self: "I choose, therefore I am."

All feminists would soundly reject the first kind of instrumentalism. Don't objectify and dehumanize women. But I'd bet most of those same feminists would just as enthusiastically embrace dualistic instrumentalism, which animates the whole genre of "sex-positive" feminism. Pornography, sadomasochism, prostitution? Nothing problematic here, if a woman elects to participate. In fact, by the sheer alchemy of her choice, those very things become a source of liberation and, to invoke the cliché, empowerment. This position is only possible to hold by depersonalizing the body, which leads to a sense of the body as a mechanism, an apparatus, an ongoing DIY project.

Once selfhood is abstracted away from material reality and characterized by unfettered choice, the human body, with its limitations, quickly becomes an obstacle to be overcome. The writer Wendell Berry articulates this retrogression in his essay "Feminism, the Body, and the Machine", in a potent paragraph worth a careful read:

> In fact, our "sexual revolution" is mostly an industrial phenomenon, in which the body is used as an idea of pleasure or a pleasure machine with the aim of "freeing" natural pleasure from natural consequence. Like any other

industrial enterprise, industrial sexuality seeks to conquer nature by exploiting it and ignoring the consequences, by denying any connection between nature and spirit or body and soul, and by evading social responsibility. The spiritual, physical, and economic costs of this "freedom" are immense.... Industrial sex, characteristically, establishes its freeness and goodness by an industrial accounting, dutifully toting up numbers of "sexual partners," orgasms, and so on, with the inevitable industrial implication that the body is somehow a limit on the idea of sex, which will be a great deal more abundant as soon as it can be done by robots.[25]

The industrial revolution and the sexual revolution are contiguous branches of the same twisted tree, the fruit of which we continue to consume eagerly, heeding that distant whisper: *take, eat, and ye shall be as gods.*

Autonomy as Temptation

When freedom-as-choice becomes the open-ended *telos* of human existence, the body quickly becomes a problem, particularly for women, because our fertile physiology ties us intimately to other bodies and to the rest of creation. In adopting this *telos*, feminism's march toward freedom has simultaneously been a flight from embodiment.

The ideal of autonomy has been central to modern feminism from its earliest days in the nineteenth century. Elizabeth Cady Stanton, foremother of the first wave, built her vision of women's liberation on a conception of the self as solitary, continually suspended in amber-like

[25] Wendell Berry, "Feminism, the Body, and the Machine", in *The Art of the Commonplace* (Berkeley, CA: Counterpoint, 2003), 76.

isolation. Woman lives alone, marooned like Robinson Crusoe on a "solitary island", where she alone is "arbiter of her own destiny". This is Stanton's feminist anthropology: the human soul in complete isolation, making "the voyage of life alone". Despite our deep "hunger of heart for love and recognition", nature teaches the grueling lesson of "self-dependence, self-protection, self-support". Stanton's picture of life and personhood is bleak. While she rightly points out the unrepeatability of each human soul, this is less a cause for awe than for desolation. There is no sense of community, reciprocal love, or interdependence. She takes what she calls the "Protestant idea" of individualism to a dismal extreme; we are more like projectiles spinning through space than interconnecting parts of a communal whole.[26]

With Sanger, this ideal of autonomy is concretely imposed on the female body, achievable only through technological control. Because bodily fertility threatens autonomy, the natural connection between sex and procreation must be severed. Simone de Beauvoir takes up this dualistic vision, making Sanger's concrete project more philosophically robust. This synergy between ground-level activism and ivory-tower speculation ensures that the value of autonomy, and its dualistic anthropology, remains entrenched in feminist theory and praxis. This does not ultimately liberate women; it causes them harm.

Several years ago, I saw a Facebook post written by a woman about why she was choosing to have an abortion. This woman was a stranger to me, but her words were

[26] Elizabeth Cady Stanton, "The Solitude of Self", address delivered to Congress, January 18, 1892, https://etc.usf.edu/lit2go/pdf/passage/4854/civil-rights-and-conflict-in-the-united-states-selected-speeches-006-solitude-of-self-address-before-the-committee-of-the-judiciary-of-the-united-states-congress-january-18-1892.pdf.

widely shared, ending up on my feed. Here is what she wrote:

> I've been waffling back and forth wondering whether to post about this, but it's an intensely personal and multitudinously painful thing I'm going through. It's important to me, though, to put myself out there as an illustration of why it's so important to have safe, ready access to abortion services. This is the second time in my life I've been on long-term, regular hormonal birth control and gotten pregnant anyway. Practicing safe and protected sex is not foolproof. Being with a loving, long-term partner does not have me jumping at the bit to be a mother. And bringing a pregnancy to term is simply not an option for me; physically, emotionally, or financially. I sincerely feel that a woman has a right to choose in any scenario.... Bodily autonomy exists, and it exists for a reason.

My first reaction to reading these words (then and still) was heartache—for this woman who was clearly in a place of pain and turmoil, and for the new human life whose value was rationalized away. I was also struck by a glaring, terrible irony of that last line: "Bodily autonomy exists, and it exists for a reason." The very reason this woman found herself in such an agonizing predicament is the fact that bodily autonomy does not, as it turns out, exist for women in the same way it does for men. Women, by their very physiology, have bodies that are open to life, bodies that welcome the stranger in before the will can bar the door. Like it or not, that is what women's bodies are designed to do. A man can have sex until he dies from exhaustion; he will never get pregnant. He will never have to agonize over whether or not to have an abortion. He is fertile, but his fertility does not open his body to the body of another. The bodily autonomy this woman claims for herself is not native to her, but must be imposed upon her body—imperfectly through contraception and, when that fails, violently through abortion.

This Facebook post, and the millions of experiences it represents, reveals something crucial: the ideal of complete sexual freedom, of "bodily autonomy", is fashioned from the norm of male embodiment. Thus for women, it is ultimately a temptation: a promise that can't deliver, a promise that hides a lie. "Take this pill," says the serpent of the new millennium, "and ye shall be as men." But a woman on the pill is still a woman, and when the illusion of autonomy collapses, it is she—and her offspring—who pay the blood price.

An ideology that envisions human beings as isolated atoms, crashing into one another in the void, is an ideology that ultimately leads to division and destruction. What would it look like to model our praxis on the norm of female embodiment? An ethos of interconnection and radical hospitality to life? An ethos that is built on the value of *integrity*, rather than *autonomy*—personal wholeness that is synergistic, opening in love to accommodate the wholeness of another. Through the lens of autonomy, pregnancy is a threat, a maladaptation. From another angle—one that sees human embodiment as integral to personhood and the person as an icon of the divine—pregnancy becomes a living mirror through which we can glimpse the qualities of God.

A pregnant woman is an image of that Love that generates all things, the Love in which we live and move and have our being. Stanton's solitary self is alone and abandoned, shipwrecked on a one-man island, "thrown wholly on herself for consolation" in the hour of "her keenest sufferings". This is a distortion. In truth, the human soul, like a child in the womb, is never alone. She is continually held in being not by her own effort or will or self-sovereignty, but by Love—Love that is the engine of all existence, Love that imprints itself onto the human form to be made visible to us. This is the heartbeat beneath things, if we can learn to hear it. Not the desolate roar of an ocean, but the steady *thrum* of a heart on fire.

†

The normalization of contraception not only altered women's material circumstances in complex and contradictory ways; it also ushered in a new conceptual paradigm, a new way of thinking about sex, embodiment, and womanhood itself. When Einar Wegener was first transfixed by the temptation of becoming a woman—again, a temptation is a promise that can't deliver—his longing to become a woman included the desire to gestate new life. By the time Christine Jorgensen embarked on a similar journey of metamorphosis, the goal posts had shifted. For many, womanhood was no longer rooted in a biological reality, but a purely social, ornamental one. To appear and act as a typical woman seemed sufficient to *become* a woman.

The separation of sexual union from procreation prompted a cascade of disconnection that has brought us to the gender bedlam of the present. Biological sex has been split off from gender, woman from female, man from male, body from the desiring will. These schisms are both conceptual and technological, facilitated by experimental treatments, hormones, and surgeries that have not been rigorously studied. Is it any wonder that today's parents don't bat an eye at the idea of dosing their children with synthetic hormones? After all, we've been doing it to our adolescent daughters already, for decades. This is just the latest chapter in the same unfolding story: the fragmentation of human personhood and the denigration of the body, all in the name of freedom.

Sex

The classic dystopian novel *Brave New World* features a totalitarian society that has completely separated human reproduction from sexual activity. Human beings are mass-produced and engineered into a caste system; from infancy, their desires are shaped and conditioned to keep them happily enslaved to the social system. Babies, naturally drawn to the beauty of the sun and flowers, are punished with electric shocks until they develop an aversion that will keep them "happy" in the industrial environment of the city. Adults are lulled into an acquiescent state by the euphoric drug soma, which provides a false happiness, a state of superficial pleasure that distracts rather than fulfills.

A social engineering feat like this depends upon the complete conquest of nature—not "nature" as in trees and bees, but nature as in human nature. Aldous Huxley was not a Christian, but the portrait he paints is deeply teleological. The dark mirror of *Brave New World* shows that the human person is not a blank slate, a *tabula rasa* awaiting social construction. The regime has to work against a pre-social nature that is continually threatening to reassert itself. The state in *Brave New World* has its own synthetic *telos* to impose, and because *telos* is connected with nature, the state must work tirelessly against human nature, systematically and violently undoing any enduring bonds of love between people, any natural inclination toward beauty and wholeness. Marriage has been eradicated, and indeed any form of committed monogamy is illicit. There are no natural family units or any family units at all—the term "mother" has become an obscenity.

Huxley's dystopia springs to my mind regularly these days. Take the other week, when I was participating in what has become a standard ritual in the twenty-first-century workplace: mandatory HR compliance training. In my ideal world, compliance training would be replaced by a simple email, sent annually, that reads: "Greetings. This is your yearly reminder from HR. Don't be a jerk." Instead, we cycle through a lengthy and tedious tour of the many possible ways of offending our colleagues, a tour that gets lengthier and more tedious each year, as the list of offenses continues to grow. This year's training, for example, included a directive to stop associating gender with biology. "Say 'pregnant people'", the slide cheerily demanded, "instead of 'pregnant women.'" As I reread this slide in disbelief, I was reminded of *Brave New World*, where technology has conquered biology, where "mother" has become a dirty word. When it comes to sex, gender, and sexuality, our world too closely mirrors Huxley's dystopia. The phrase "pregnant woman" is a microaggression, a slur, because it makes the now-transgressive assumption that only women can get pregnant.

How did we get here? What is being rewritten? What has been unlearned? To answer these questions, we must delve into the concepts of "sex" and "gender", map the shifting meanings of these words, and reanchor them in reality. That will be the focus of the following two chapters, as we take a hard look at biological sex and gender in turn.

Essential Potential

From the second wave onward, feminism has had an ongoing problem with both resisting and depending upon a stable definition of woman. On the one hand, the very term "feminism" indicates a focus on *femmes*, women. Yet feminism has also been marked by a deep suspicion toward the idea of a universal, timeless understanding of what a woman is.

There is some good reason for this. Various cultures and historical moments have featured dehumanizing definitions of woman, denying women basic rights and access to education on the grounds that women are intellectually deficient and only good for producing offspring, ideally sons. Feminists have also pointed out the difficulty of finding a definition that is capacious enough to include all women: What is the foundational denominator to which we can point? We can't point to physical features, because that would exclude women who have had hysterectomies, women who can grow full beards, women who tower over the average man. We can't point to motherhood, because not all women are mothers. We can't point to character traits—compassion, gentleness—because we can all think of women who don't exemplify those traits.

Notice how this line of thought is circular? I am rejecting definitions of "woman" on the grounds that they don't include *all women*. I am taking for granted, in my evaluations, that there is such a being as "woman", and then I'm searching for a way to articulate exactly what distinguishes that being from other beings. What is the whatness, the *quiddity*, of woman?

The idea that all women share some intrinsic property that characterizes "woman-ness" is called *essentialism*. An essentialist perspective affirms that men and women are fundamentally, or essentially, different. This doesn't have to mean that they are polar opposites, different in every way, but rather that there is some distinguishing feature that all women have and all men do not, and vice versa. In gender theory, essentialism is often contrasted with social

constructionism, which is the idea that there are no differences between men and women at the level of being; any
differences we perceive are products of society and culture.

Feminist thought, for reasons described above, is over-
whelmingly antiessentialist, and to escape the tension
caused by rejecting essentialism on the one hand, while
retaining a woman-centered movement on the other,
many feminists appeal to *nominalism*. Nominalism—which
evokes the notion of *nom* or "name"—is the idea that we
can group things together in name only, without appealing
to a universal essence that transcends culture. I can say, for
example, that women exist, because the idea of woman
exists as a mental and social construct. Feminist theorists
write of using essentialism nominally and "strategically",
appealing to a catch-all category when it suits, rejecting
the category when it doesn't, and resisting any attempts to
define that category.

I was caught in this nominalist-essentialist loop as a college student. I was first drawn to feminism by an avowedly
essentialist impulse: I saw my womanhood as an integral
part of my identity, and I felt a longing to understand
and embrace my dignity *as a woman* specifically. At first
glance, feminism seemed to offer a space where I could do
exactly that. I did not expect to have to reject the idea of
womanhood in order to find my dignity. Once I became
immersed in feminist thought, however, I quickly picked
up on the fact that essentialism was an unforgiveable feminist sin.

I remember sitting in a feminist philosophy class as a
college senior, bandying around possible definitions of
"woman" with my classmates, always coming up short. I
kept wanting to appeal to the body, to female biology, but
was admittedly stumped by the exceptions. Are women
who have had hysterectomies no longer women? I could

see that idea was clearly absurd, but I couldn't articulate *why*. Even so, I remained a closet essentialist, playing the nominalism card as needed, secretly holding on to the idea that womanhood was a core part of my identity, that "woman" named something fundamental and real, something deeper than a social fiction.

I tried to confess this once to a male classmate. We were both taking the feminist philosophy class, both card-carrying, self-avowed feminists. One day after class, he asked me to articulate my perspective. How do I understand my identity as a woman, he asked? I don't remember what I said; I only remember that I spoke honestly, and his response was incredulous: "You can't think that! That's *essentialism!*" The irony of having a male classmate reject my perspective in order to toe the feminist line is not lost on me. His response shows how the rejection of essentialism is a *premise* in most feminist philosophy, rather than a well-reasoned conclusion. I had only been a feminist for a hot minute, and already I was a heretic.

The tool I lacked in my analytical toolbox was this: the crucial distinction between potentiality and actuality. I first encountered these concepts in the work of the philosopher and theologian Saint Thomas Aquinas, who in turn adapted them from Aristotle. *Potentiality* (also called "potency") refers to any inherent potential or possibility a thing has. *Actuality* (also called "act") is the realization or actualization of that inherent possibility. Let's play with some examples.

Before I sat down to write this morning, I was looking at some of my daughter's worksheets from kindergarten. She's just learning how to arrange letters into words, based on sound. On one worksheet, she'd listed characters from the Christmas story: MRE, AJL, CING—a.k.a. Mary, Angel, King. There's something awe-inducing about seeing her oversized, shaky, and often backwards letters being arranged to create intelligible words. There is a potential within her—the potential to read, to write, to reason, to develop language—that is being drawn into actuality, and it is thrilling to see it unfold in real time. She's been in kindergarten for only two months, and already she's beginning to write and to read.

My cat, Kafka, also has some linguistic abilities. At least, he can communicate pretty well. Like his namesake, Kafka is full of angst; he meows loudly whenever he needs something, usually water, food, or attention, and he has a particularly deep and proud yowl to signal the presentation of a trophy, usually the corpse of a dead rat. Despite his intelligence and ability to communicate, if I sent Kafka to kindergarten, he would never learn to read. I could keep him in school until his nine lives ran out, and it would just never happen, because he does not have the inherent potential to develop literacy. There are plenty of animals more intelligent than Kafka, but none of them could do what my five-year-old daughter is now doing, because they lack the potential to do so, by their very nature.

How does this help us define "woman"? In my prior and failed attempts to settle on a definition, I was working only with the idea of *actuality*, fumbling to find a characteristic that would be *actually* true for all women at all times. I held the common-sense intuition that a woman is an adult human female but was unsure how to respond to the inevitable what-aboutery that springs up in response to any proposed definition: What about infertile women? What about postmenopausal women? What about women who've had mastectomies and hysterectomies? What about women with a Y chromosome?

Potentiality solves this problem. A woman is the kind of human being whose body is organized around the potential to gestate new life. This *potentiality* that belongs to female-ness is always present, even if there is some kind of con-dition, such as age or disease, that prevents that potential from being actualized. The very category of "infertility" does not undermine this definition, but affirms it. A male human who cannot get pregnant is not deemed "infertile", because he never had that potential in the first place. A woman who cannot get pregnant does have that poten-tial, and so she is considered infertile. Infertility names the often painful and devastating inability to actualize one's procreative potential.

Maybe I have found a well-armored definition of woman, but doesn't this definition reduce people to reproductive function? Isn't that dehumanizing? The first response I have to this objection is that this definition is not about *function* per se, but about innate *potential*. This is an important distinction, because it affirms the reality that women who do not procreate are still fully women.

My second response is to call to mind again that guid-ing principle of thinking like a Catholic: when we talk about people, we are always talking about bodies *and* souls, physical-spiritual beings. Our consideration of woman-hood must include bodily sex, but must also extend beyond it to consider the whole person. That's the lively tension we need to inhabit: to remain rooted in the body but not reduced to the body.

I recently saw a tweet from the brand Tampax that pro-claimed, "not all people with periods are women. Let's celebrate the diversity of people who bleed!"[1] This echoes the worldview behind the HR training I took that man-dated the phrase "pregnant people" rather than "pregnant

---

[1] Tampax US (@Tampax), Twitter, September 15, 2020, https://twitter.com/Tampax/status/1305952342504767491.

women". I've seen similar permutations elsewhere: people with a cervix, chest-feeders, birthing parents—linguistic somersaults to speak about female bodies without using the term *woman*. *This* strikes me as the dehumanizing, function-based approach. Instead of a term that evokes an integrated, personal entity—"woman"—we have phrases based on function and then loosely attached to person-hood, which is necessarily delimiting. "Birthing parent" is narrowly focused on the function of giving birth; "mother" evokes that role, but blooms far beyond it, encompassing so much more than one singular event or function.

It is the gender paradigm that employs function-based categorization rather than person-based categorization. By divorcing femaleness from the concept of "woman", this paradigm creates a schism between body and identity. Instead of body–identity integration, we are left with frag-mentation, a picture of the human person like a Potato Head doll: a hollow, neuter shell that comes with an assortment of rearrangeable parts.

The Science of Sex

Now that we have a working definition of woman that is connected to femaleness, let's tackle some of the mis-guided assumptions about biological sex in our culture. One of my finer teaching moments in gender theory was successfully luring my students into the following thought-trap. During one of our class discussions, I noticed some students parroting the line that biological sex is "assigned" at birth by doctors and parents rather than identified or recognized. "Wait a second", I said. "Is sexual orientation innate, something we are born with?" My students nod-ded readily. This is well-established dogma. "And you're also saying that biological sex is a social construct, a category arbitrarily 'assigned' at birth?" More vigorous nods. "How is that possible? Aren't those claims contradictory? How is it possible to have an *innate* attraction to something that is merely a social construct?" Aha. In that millisecond, I saw a brief glimmer of light cut through the postmodern haze. Even if they quickly turned away, they had at least recognized the contradiction.

The bizarre idea that biological sex is "assigned" at birth for everyone is one of several myths about sex that have gained widespread acceptance in our time. These myths tend to cluster together, like one trapdoor that opens into another. Once you accept one myth as true, you quickly freefall down the rabbit hole. The first trapdoor is this idea: sex is not binary but a spectrum. This leads to the notion that the categories "male" and "female" are social constructs, rather than terms that correspond to an objective truth about human nature. If sex is a construct, then the labels "girl" and "boy" are indeed "assigned" by doctors, who thus create the illusion of a binary. Lastly, if birth sex is not identified *from* the body, but projected *onto* the body, then sex can be changed.

The gateway into this spiral of myths is the contention that sex is not binary—in other words, the contention that there are more than two sexes or that sex is a spectrum. The question is: Do we have good evidence to support this contention?

Come! Let's take a magical mystery tour through the science of sex.

Human bodies are teleologically organized according to our distinct role in reproducing the species. The structure of our bodies is arranged to produce either large sex cells or small sex cells. These sex cells are called gametes. Large gametes are ova, and small gametes are sperm. A physiology arranged to produce ova is female, and a physiology arranged to produce sperm is male. This twofold distinction between large and small gametes is stable and universal, not only throughout the human species, but also among *all* plant and animal species that reproduce sexually.

There is no such thing as a third gamete or a spectrum of possible gametes. This invariable feature of our humanity ties us intimately to the rest of creation. When the gametes combine, they can create a new member of the species. The sex binary, then, is the necessary foundation for the continued transmission of human existence. (If it's just a construct, we're in trouble.)

Rather than arbitrarily assigned at birth, a baby's sex is determined at conception, through the SRY gene (or its absence). This gene is the master switch of sexual differentiation; if triggered, the SRY gene initiates a process of sexual development toward the production of male gametes. Without successful SRY activation, the gonads of a developing baby become ovaries, which are structured to produce female gametes.

If the science is clear, and the sex binary in humans has existed for millions of years—why are we suddenly facing the novel notion of sex as a spectrum? In the following chapter, I will sketch out a possible genealogy for this idea; here, I would like to respond to two central arguments behind the spectrum hypothesis.

This is by far the most common rejoinder I hear: "Sex is not a binary. *Intersex people exist.*" Foot soldiers of the gender brigade always make sure to carry the intersex card in a ready holster and are quick on the draw. This reflexive reference to intersex is a great rhetorical move, because most people don't know enough about the topic to make a cogent response. The term is used in such a way to suggest that "intersex" refers to something completely outside the male/female binary, like some third sex or non-sex category of persons who are neither male nor female, or somehow both male *and* female. In this way, the intersex trump card is used to erase the fundamental and stable reality of biological sex, in order to justify the idea that sex is a construct and open the door to limitless self-identification.

The term "intersex" is an umbrella term encompassing a range of conditions that disrupt the development of certain sexual characteristics. Despite its prevalence in the gender theory world, the term is imprecise and often misused. Medical literature tends to use the term "disorders of sexual development" (DSDs). I have also seen "differences of sexual development" and "variations of sexual development" (VSDs). I prefer the term "congenital conditions of sexual development" (CCSDs), which is medically precise and avoids the language of "disorder" that some find stigmatizing. Moreover, including the word "congenital" helpfully limits the range of conditions; while late onset disruptions of sexual development can occur, these do not result in sexual ambiguity at birth. If "intersex" is used to invoke a category *in between* the sexes, it is a misnomer. However, the label can be accurately used when referring to a biologically based variation *within* maleness or femaleness.

I first encountered the concept of intersexuality in graduate school, when I was studying gender theory. I came across the book *Sexing the Body* by biologist Anne Fausto-Sterling and found it utterly fascinating. I had never done a deep dive into the complexities of sexual development before, and her radical conclusions blew my hair back. I used this book as a primary source in the culminating project for my master's coursework, in which I argued that science itself is a gendered discipline with an inherent masculine bias (an entertaining but ultimately flawed line of argumentation).

Fausto-Sterling is the fairy godmother of the intersex gambit, that tokenizing reference to intersex people used to dismantle the idea of a sex binary. Her work is also the origin of common misconceptions about CCSDs, such as the idea that these conditions are as common as having red hair. In a coauthored article "How Sexually Dimorphic Are We?", Fausto-Sterling *et al.* argue that sex should be understood as a continuum, rather than a binary, and a key part of their argument is the notion that intersex conditions are fairly common, occurring in as many as 1.7 per 100 live births (1.7%).[2] They arrive at this number through an overly expansive definition of intersex, one that includes any "individual who deviates from the Platonic ideal of physical dimorphism at the chromosomal, genital, gonadal, or hormonal levels."[3] This capacious definition would include conditions such as polycystic ovarian syndrome (PCOS), a hormonal disorder that occurs when a woman produces excess androgen, or Klinefelter syndrome, when a man has an extra X chromosome. (It might even include me! My body hair situation is decidedly *not* in line with the Platonic ideal.) While these conditions may lead to fertility problems, they do not cause sexual ambiguity. A woman with PCOS is clearly female, and a man with Klinefelter is clearly male, often unaware of his chromosomal variation until he attempts to have children.

In fact, the five most common conditions that Faust-Sterling categorizes as "intersex" do not actually involve instances of sexual ambiguity. When we restrict the category to include only such cases, the number plummets to 0.018%—a figure one hundred times *lower* than

[2] M. Blackless et al., "How Sexually Dimorphic Are We? Review and Synthesis", *American Journal of Human Biology* 12, no. 2 (2000): 151–66, https://pubmed.ncbi.nlm.nih.gov/11534012/.

[3] Blackless et al., "How Sexually Dimorphic?", 161.

Fausto-Sterling's estimate.[4] Rather than the inflated rate of 1.7 out of 100 births, CCSDs occur in fewer than 2 out of 10,000 births. This is a crucial point to understand: *the vast majority of individuals often categorized as intersex are unambiguously male or female*, even if the presentation of maleness or femaleness is atypical in some way.

Take the condition of vaginal agenesis, which Fausto-Sterling categorizes as intersex. Baby girls born with this condition have a vagina that is not fully developed, along with fully functioning ovaries, which lead to female sex characteristics. In Fausto-Sterling's logic, a girl with vaginal agenesis is not "really" female. Ironically, her attempt to critique the Platonic ideals of maleness and femaleness actually *reinforces* those ideals, by exempting those with variations in sexual development from the sex binary altogether.

Given the fact that sexual development is a process and at each stage of the process, things can go awry, I am actually surprised how *rare* cases of genuine sexual ambiguity are. I'm not surprised such cases exist; rather, I'm surprised there are so few. Statistically speaking, sex is readily recognizable at birth for 99.98% of human beings. That is remarkably consistent. In the remaining outlying cases, the reality of sex is still present but must be more carefully discerned—not for curiosity's sake, but in order to support the person's physical health. This is not because those individuals are neither male nor female, but rather because their developmental pathways of becoming male or female took some unexpected turns.

Discerning sex in these individuals entails looking at multiple factors taken together: karyotype (chromosomes);

[4] Leonard Sax, "How Common Is Intersex? A Response to Anne Fausto-Sterling", *Journal of Sex Research* 39, no. 3 (2002): 174–78, https://pubmed.ncbi.nlm.nih.gov/12476264/.

phenotype (genitalia); gonads (ovaries or testes); internal structures that support gamete production; and hormones. Sexual ambiguity occurs when the phenotype is not readily classifiable as male or female or when the karyotype is not consistent with the phenotype, as in cases of complete androgen insensitivity syndrome (CAIS).[5] Overly broad use of the term "intersex" tends to privilege karyotype and phenotype, while overlooking gamete production and the structure of the body as a whole. In the face of ambiguity in these first two factors, genderists tend to conclude prematurely that the verdict is in: the sex binary is false. Popular memes, such as the Genderbread Person, portray sex on a spectrum and define sex as a mix-and-match assemblage of "genitalia, body shape, voice pitch, body hair, hormones, chromosomes, etc." Gamete production is not mentioned at all, even though this is the foundation of biological sex.

This reflects a common error: reducing biological sex to secondary sex characteristics—seeing sex as merely about genital appearance or breast development. The gender paradigm fundamentally misunderstands what sex is, confusing cause with effect. Secondary sex characteristics develop as a *consequence* of sex; they are the effect, rather than the cause.

This misunderstanding is often perpetuated to reach a desired conclusion: the notion that a person can change his or her sex. If sex is defined by secondary characteristics like genital appearance and voice depth, then changing sex *is* possible, through surgery and synthetic hormones. If, however, sex is fundamentally about how the body is organized in relation to gamete production—a potentiality that cannot be endowed by a scalpel—then the undeniable

[5] See Sax, "How Common Is Intersex?"

truth is this: it is *not* possible to change one's sex, because sex is constitutive of the whole person.

When faced with ambiguity at the level of phenotype and karyotype, the best response is not to shrug and embrace the spectrum, but to continue the discernment of sex by looking at the anatomical structures that support either large gamete production or small gamete production. Although the term "hermaphrodite" used to be applied to cases of sexual ambiguity, this is a dehumanizing misnomer. Hermaphrodites are species that do not have separate sexes, such as snails and slugs; instead, each member of the species has the ability to produce both large and small gametes and can thus take on either the "male" or "female" role in reproduction. For this kind of species, hermaphroditic reproduction is the norm. Human biology, on the other hand, does not support this mode of reproduction. In the rarest CCSD, an individual can develop both ovarian and testicular tissue, but even in this case, he or she will produce one gamete or the other, not both. There have only been about five hundred documented cases of an ovotesticular CCSD in medical history, and there is no direct evidence in the literature of a hermaphroditic human being, someone able to produce both small and large gametes.[6]

When all the dimensions of sex are taken into account, sex can be discerned in each human being. To conclude otherwise is to exclude some individuals from a reality in which we all participate. This kind of thinking has unintended and harmful consequences, ones that lead to bodily violation.

---

[6] See Meltem Özdemir et al., "Ovotesticular Disorder of Sex Development: An Unusual Presentation", *Journal of Clinical Imaging Science* 9, no. 34 (2019), https://www.ncbi.nlm.nih.gov/pmc/articles/PMC6737443/.

Bodily Integrity

Despite its flaws, one of the most valuable aspects of Fausto-Sterling's work is her critique of infant genital mutilation (IGM), medically unnecessary surgeries on infants born with CCSDs. This used to be standard medical practice. If a baby was born with atypical or ambiguous genitalia, the reaction was to whip out the scalpel and attempt to sculpt more normal-looking genitals. An infant girl born with an enlarged clitoris (clitoromegaly) might be subjected to unnecessary genital surgery to make the clitoris appear more normal. Surgeries like this, which are purely cosmetic, can lead to reduced sexual function and sensation.

Even more disturbing: a healthy infant of one sex might be categorized and raised as the opposite sex, simply because of the external appearance of the genitals. This is the situation in which the phrase "assigned sex" is accurate: a baby boy with a micropenis might have been surgically altered and raised as a girl, simply because his male genitalia didn't match the norm. It is easier to surgically mimic the appearance of a vagina, so infants with ambiguous genitalia were more regularly designated "female", regardless of overall bodily structure. I remember this chilling line from Fausto-Sterling's book, which she attributed to a surgeon: "You can make a hole, but you can't build a pole."

The animating problem behind the practice of IGM is an idealization of how male and female genitalia should *look*. The emphasis is on cosmetic appearance, rather than respect for the integrity of the body and how the body is organized as a whole.

Intersex activism first arose in the 1990s—not as an attempt to dismantle the sex binary, but rather to end harmful medical practices and raise awareness of CCSDs. The Intersex Society of North America (ISNA) successfully advocated for groundbreaking changes in the healthcare system. Clinical guidelines published in 2006 established new protocols for responding to infants with CCSDs, including a more cautious approach to surgical intervention, with attention to bodily function and medical necessity rather than appearance. After these successes, ISNA disbanded in 2008, which is around the time I first learned about intersex conditions in graduate school. At the time, it seemed like we were entering a new era of respecting the dignity and bodily integrity of people with CCSDs, but the mainstreaming of postmodern gender theory is reversing that progress.

Proponents of the sex spectrum claim to be allies of people with CCSDs, and I am sure most are acting in good faith. But the knee-jerk invocation "Intersex people exist!" is used to cast doubt on the reality of biological sex rather than to cultivate an awareness of the unique circumstances and needs of people with CCSDs. Ironically, postmodern genderists fall into the same error as those surgeons who performed unneeded surgeries: they place undue emphasis on idealized stereotypes of how men and women should *look*. If we refer to the Gender Unicorn—an Internet meme that distills postmodern gender theory into a cartoonish diagram—there are three options listed for "sex assigned at birth": male, female, and other/intersex. This meme classifies "intersex" as something *other* than male or female, a mischaracterization commonly found in activist rhetoric. Unfortunately, this way of framing CCSDs dehumanizes intersex individuals by insisting that any deviations from idealized norms are not "really" male or female, but "other". In this understanding, a girl born with atypical genitalia is expelled from the category "female" altogether and placed in some amorphous third category or marooned along a spectrum between maleness and femaleness.

Increasingly, the term "intersex" is invoked as a "got-cha!" card in debates about transgender identities. The addition of an "I" to the ever expansive LGBTQIA+ acronym conflates, in a reductive and unhelpful way, the very different situations of individuals with CCSDs and trans-identifying people. One notable point of tension is the question of bodily integrity.

The intersex activist effort has focused on ending muti-lating surgeries, valuing health and wholeness over ideal-ized appearance and preserving the integrity of the body in whatever form it comes. These efforts are in tension with transgender activism, which advocates invasive surgeries on healthy bodies, values cosmetic appearance over health and bodily function, and does not respect the integrity of the body as a good that should be preserved. The proce-dures that intersex activists describe as "mutilations" are the same procedures that trans activists insist are good and necessary, even for minors. IGMs are rightly decried not simply because they are nonconsensual—although this is a crucial factor—but also because they do unnecessary harm to the body. For the trans activist, the integrity of the body matters *only when I want it to matter*. The underlying fantasy of postmodernity is that we have control over our nature, that we are the masters, the gods, the makers. Rather than affirming that fantasy, people with CCSDs expose it as false, because they are reckoning with bodily realities out-side of their control.

There have been some attempts to categorize trans-identifying people as intersex, usually by appealing to the idea of a congenital "brain sex" that does not align with bodily sex. Several neuroimaging studies have explored the hypothesis that the brains of trans-identified peo-ple bear greater similarity to the brains of their professed gender than their natal sex. There are problems with this theory on three distinct levels. First of all, there is no solid evidence for an association between brain structure and trans-identification. The neuroimaging studies that exist are small and very limited and generate inconclusive and contradictory results.[7] Secondly, *even if* we had solid evidence for these structural and functional brain differences, due to neuroplasticity, the causal relationship would remain unclear. In other words, it would be impossible to tell if such differences were congenital and led to trans-identification or if trans-identification and transition had rewired the brain.[8] Thirdly, *even if* we had solid evidence for this association *and* evidence that it is congenital like an intersex condition, we still arrive at another problem: Why should sex be defined according to neuroanatomy rather than the presence of a healthy reproductive system, when sex is fundamentally a reproductive category? Redefining

---

[7] A 2016 report by physician Lawrence Mayer and psychiatrist Paul McHugh published in *The New Atlantis* gives a comprehensive overview of brain imagining studies, concluding that the studies "show inconclusive evidence and mixed findings regarding the brains of transgender adults. Brain-activation patterns in these studies do not offer sufficient evidence for drawing sound conclusions about possible associations between brain activation and sexual identity or arousal. The results are conflicting and confusing." See Mayer and McHugh, "Special Report on Sexuality and Gender: Findings from the Biological, Psychological, and Social Sciences", *The New Atlantis* 50 (Fall 2016). For additional, more recent studies, which also provide conflicting results, see S. Mueller et al., "A Structural Magnetic Resonance Imaging Study in Transgender Persons on Cross-Sex Hormone Therapy", *Neuroendocrinology* 105 (2017); Carme Uribe et al., "Brain Network Interactions in Transgender Individuals with Gender Incongruence", *NeuroImage* 211 (2020): article no. 116613, https://doi.org/10.1016/j.neuroimage.2020.116613.

[8] One 2018 peer-reviewed study concludes: "Given the close relationship and interaction between culture, behavior and brain, the individual's brain adapts itself to the new condition (culture) and concepts and starts to alter its function and structure." See M. R. Mohammadi and Ali Khaleghi, "Transsexualism: A Different Viewpoint to Brain Changes", *Clinical Psychopharmacology and Neuroscience* 16, no. 2 (2018): 136–43, https://www.ncbi.nlm.nih.gov/pmc/articles/PMC5953012/.

sex according to brain structure and function would mean that *any* woman or man whose neuroimages deviate from the norm is not "really" a woman or a man at all. I am not denying that some cases of sexual incongruence might have a neurological basis. That is certainly possible. What I am disputing is the idea of "brain sex", which is not supported by evidence and contradicts a basic biological understanding of what sex is.

Let me gather the important threads here.

Sex is not a spectrum but a stable binary—not only in the human species but in all sexually reproductive plant and animal species. There is no third sex. There is no spectrum of possible sexes.

In the process of sexual development, there can be variations that lead to atypical manifestations of maleness and femaleness. In 99.98% of these cases, sex is readily recognizable as unambiguously male or female. Categorizing these individuals as "intersex" or "other" leads to the idea that some women are "more" or "less" female based on how closely their bodies approximate the norm. Am I "less" female because I have more facial and body hair than the ideal? Am I less of a woman because, as I was told in high school, my legs look like a man's legs? This way of thinking draws a narrow, superficial box around maleness and femaleness and demeans anyone who falls outside its bounds.

The 0.02% of cases where sex is not readily identifiable do not represent a third sex or points on a spectrum. Even here, sex is present and must be discerned with an attention to the whole person and supporting his or her physical health. These extremely rare situations are by definition unique and particular, and the focus must be on the individual's specific needs. Some CCSDs, like other congenital conditions, require medical attention and management, in order to maintain bodily health and integrity.

Co-opting the existence of intersex people to promote a postmodern understanding of sex and gender is unjust. The most humanizing and precise way to view CCSDs is to understand these conditions not as exceptions from the sex binary, but as variations within the binary. We need to make room *within* the boxes of male and female for a diverse range of body types and personalities. We do not need to abolish the boxes altogether.

Body as Sacrament

I've been spending a fair bit of time here on the biological plane. It's important to understand what sex is, and how sexual development unfolds, in order to be able to counter the postmodern myths. That can't be the extent of our discussion, however, if we're thinking from a Christian perspective. Our consideration of sex and gender must be attuned to the holistic and sacred reality of the *person*—the person as an integrated unity of body and soul. We must follow a path of contemplation that sees the various dimensions of personhood in order to receive the miracle of each person. This is a path that moves toward integration, from disorder to wholeness. The postmodern approach to sex and gender runs in the opposite direction, into fragmentation, a piecemeal self, where body and psyche and desire are split off from one another and rearrangeable—where the body is not the foundation of personal identity, but rather its lifeless tool.

In contrast, the personalist approach allows us to see each human being as a *person*, rather than a collection of ever-proliferating labels, and, more importantly, to attune our awareness to the sacramentality of every human body. Bodies are not "just" bodies. Bodies are persons made manifest.

The sacramental principle is always at work: the visible reveals the invisible. The body reveals to us the eternal and divine reality of the person—a reality that can only break into the tangible, sensible world through embodiment.

That is how God enters into our world and reveals himself, through the incarnational reality of Christ, who became a body that we might know and love the invisible God. The Incarnation is both a historical moment, a plot on the timeline of the world story, and an eternal moment. The divine Person who quickened in the womb of Mary is also the Person who, in the Eucharist, clothes himself in the molecules of wine and bread, that he might be placed on our tongues and engulfed by our hearts. This mystery—the sacramental mystery of the Incarnation—should frame our vision of all that is.

Too easily, we lose sight of this mystery; we allow our vision to contract, to become superficial and self-serving. We fall into the perennial error of seeing some human bodies as not-quite-human and thus disposable, cast out of the circle of what's seen and what's valued.

This time-worn tendency is on glaring display in Flannery O'Connor's story "A Temple of the Holy Ghost". Told from the perspective of an imaginative child who fantasizes about heroic martyrdom while skimping on her prayers, this story casts a bright beam on the dignity and sacramentality of the intersex person.

There's a fair in town, one with a Ferris wheel, merry-go-round, and "closed tent" exhibits for adults only. The child protagonist hears two older girls talking in hushed tones about what they saw in one of the tents: a "freak" that was "a man and woman both".[9] This person had "a particular name", but the girls don't remember it, instead

---

[9] Flannery O'Connor, "Temple of the Holy Ghost", in *The Complete Stories* (New York: Farrar, Straus and Giroux, 1997), 245.

using demeaning terms like "you-know-what" and the excising pronoun "It".[10]

The child, being a child, is not allowed into the closed exhibit, but her robust imagination embellishes the scant details provided by the older girls. She imagines the exhibit like a tent revival, the intersex person as preacher: "God made me thisaway ... God done this to me and I praise him." The people murmur, "Amen. Amen." The preaching goes on: "Raise yourself up. A temple of the Holy Ghost. You! You are God's temple, don't you know? God's Spirit has a dwelling in you, don't you know? ... A temple of God is a holy thing. Amen. Amen. I am a temple of the Holy Ghost."[11]

This fantasy of a communal worship service led by the intersex person stands in stark opposition to how the town's religious authorities actually respond. By the end of the story, we learn that the fair has been closed prematurely, after the town preachers do an inspection and tell the police to "shut it on down".[12] Rather than whispering "amen" and praising God for his handiwork, the townsfolk say "begone".

In one of her personal letters, O'Connor explains how that intersex character is the only person who approaches holiness in the story. She writes, "as near as I get to saying what purity is in this story is saying that it is an acceptance of what God wills for us, an acceptance of our individual circumstances."[13] Only the intersex person displays that spiritual wisdom, the purity of self-acceptance, a purity made even more remarkable in the face of ostracism.

The closing section of the story centers on another kind of exhibition: Eucharistic Adoration, the Catholic practice

---

[10] O'Connor, "Temple of the Holy Ghost", 245.

[11] O'Connor, "Temple of the Holy Ghost", 246.

[12] O'Connor, "Temple of the Holy Ghost", 248.

[13] Flannery O'Connor, *The Collected Works* (New York: Library of America, 1988), 976.

of sitting in reverence before a consecrated Host, the small circle of bread that has been changed by the Holy Spirit into the Body of Christ. This form of Christ's Body is unexpected, dazzling our assumptions about what should be.

When the child sees the raised monstrance with the Body of Christ "shining ivory-colored in the center of it", she thinks again about the person from the closed tent, and she hears that person say, "This is the way He wanted me to be."[14]

Through this religious imagery, O'Connor deftly portrays two truths simultaneously. First, the undeniable fact that people with unexpected bodies are often shunned, scapegoated, and dehumanized. This is still happening. Despite its so-called progressivism, the current portrayal of intersex people as neither men nor women is simply the latest version of this othering—the updated, politically permissible way of saying "freak" and "It".

Secondly, O'Connor is drawing a profound parallel between the intersex person and Christ himself. Like Christ, the person's identity baffles and confuses the crowd. Like Christ, the person is shunned, mocked, and rejected. Like Christ in Adoration, the person's body is on display. Just as Christ's divine personhood is made visible by his eucharistic Body, the intersex body is likewise a revelation, a sacramental image of the living God and a temple of his indwelling Spirit. The extended parallel highlights the hypocrisy, the inherent contradiction, of adoring the Body of Christ, his divinity and humanity— while denigrating the intersex body, which carries divine dignity.

This story calls us to take a posture of adoration, to see all of reality, and every human being, through the

---

[14] O'Connor, "Temple of the Holy Ghost", 248.

illuminating mystery of the Incarnation. Each body is an icon of Christ; each body is a sacrament, revealing to us the sacred and unrepeatable mystery of the person.

Let our knees tremble in wonder at this.

Amen, amen.

Gender

A colleague once expressed to me her dismay that a student in my gender theory class was unable to articulate the difference between sex and gender. I found this oddly affirming: this student had rightly picked up on the fact that those two terms do not have fixed meanings in gender theory, and certainly not in the culture at large.

What *is* the difference? Are "sex" and "gender" interchangeable synonyms? Do they reflect a gnostic split between body (sex) and soul (gender)? Do they signify the interplay between biology and society in human identity? Depending upon the context, the words "sex" and "gender" can evoke any and all of those meanings. Why? Because, in a nutshell, we are deeply confused about what it means to be a body. We no longer know who we are as sexed beings, and this is mirrored in our language.

Perhaps more importantly, the meanings we hitch to those words reflect, whether intended or not, specific philosophical assumptions about what it means to be a human person. These meanings are continuing to shift at an astonishing rate. As a Christian, I believe that the proper response to any human person is always love and respect, but this does not exempt our culture's *idea* of human personhood from scrutiny. What is needed at this juncture is a hard look at, to borrow Chesterton's phrase, "the idea of the idea" of gender in our time.

The Eclipse of Sex

In the last century, our understanding of sex and gender has undergone a monumental shift—or, more specifically, *two* shifts. To trace the story of gender's cultural ascendancy, I have to describe a twofold revolution: first, the erosion of the old framework, in which bodily sex referred to the person as a whole and was characterized by generative roles, and secondly, the emergence of an alternate framework, one centered on the inherently unstable concept of gender.

Before the middle of the twentieth century, the word "gender" lived discreetly in the realm of grammar as a basic word denoting a category, kind, or class. One might find references to "the feminine gender" as a synonym for womankind, but it was more customary to speak of *words* having gender, as words do in various languages, such as French and Russian. The word "sex", in contrast, has referred exclusively to male and female differences in living beings, whether plants or animals, since at least the 1300s, only more recently taking on the additional meaning of a shorthand for "sexual intercourse"—a phrase that signals the bodily nature of "sex" and its connection to reproduction.

The predominant use of the word "sex" to indicate manhood or womanhood reveals a particular understanding of these terms. Sex, a reality expressed in the body, is seen as something innate, a given, a fact of nature recognized at birth, and one that provides the foundation of a person's identity. As discussed previously, this represents what gender theorists would call an *essentialist* understanding of sexed identity. In this view, human beings come into existence in two distinct forms, male and female, and this difference of sex occurs on the level of being itself; it is ontological, intrinsic, part of the *essence* of the person.

Perhaps most importantly, this intrinsic sexed identity is not merely about external *appearance* but also intimately connected to procreative *function*, one's generative potential as a male or female. This understanding of sex stretches back to the beginning of Western thought; we see this in Aristotle's *Generation of Animals*, for example: a male is the animal that generates in another, and a female is the animal that generates within herself. This does not mean, as discussed in the previous chapter, that a man or woman who cannot procreate is not truly a man or woman. In that prior discussion, we explored how human bodies are structured to support either small or large gamete production. Understood in this way, sex reflects a reproductive capacity, one that is not reducible to genitals or chromosomes but characterizes the organism as a whole.

How did we arrive at this cultural moment, where bodily sex is no longer considered to be integral to personhood, but is ornamental, easily altered, a fiction "assigned" at birth? I'd like to argue that this new understanding of sex can be traced, in large part, to two related innovations in the mid-twentieth century: first, the widespread embrace of contraception, which then enabled a newly expansive concept of "gender" to emerge.

It is difficult to underestimate the impact of widespread contraception on our culture, in terms of both thought and practice. The thread I'd like to take up here is how contraception reshaped our shared cultural understanding of the meaning of the sexed body. In our imagination, reproduction has receded into the background. Our procreative capacities are seen as incidental to manhood and womanhood, rather than an integral aspect—indeed, the defining feature—of those very identities. We live and move and have our trysts in a contraceptive society, where the visible sexual markers of our bodies no longer gesture toward new life, but signal the prospect of sterile pleasure.

That has become the meaning of the body in our time, as exemplified by the work of Michel Foucault, the god-father of contemporary gender theory.

Foucault's four-volume work *A History of Sexuality* begins by describing how, in the Victorian era, sexuality was taken hostage by "the conjugal family", who "absorbed it into the serious function of reproduction."[1] Ostensibly, Foucault is writing in a descriptive mode, tracing a conceptual history of sex, but from the very first page, it is clear that he is working from the assumption that human sexuality is only secondarily or even artificially about reproduction. Foucault writes this opus in the 1970s and '80s, from a cultural context where contraception has been normalized, a context that is primed to embrace a new understanding of sexuality, divorced from procreation altogether. Theologian Angela Franks aptly describes the Foucauldian view of sex, which now holds supremacy in our culture. Sex, for Foucault, is about "bodies and pleasures". If fertility no longer matters, "it does not matter whether the bodies are male or female; they are all just raw material for anonymous couplings." Our "age of contraception" has ushered in a "depersonalized view of the body" and a "world in which female fertility just does not fit."[2]

I want to extend Franks' analysis here to underscore a further ramification, mentioned in the previous two chapters. If "man" and "woman" refer to our generative potentiality, changing one's sex is an impossibility, because a man cannot physically adopt the procreative role of a female, and vice versa. But now that bodily sex has been divorced from procreative potential, reduced to appearance

---

[1] Michel Foucault, *A History of Sexuality: An Introduction*, vol. 1 (New York: Knopf Doubleday, 2012), 3.

[2] Angela Franks, "Humane Vitae in Light of the War Against Female Fertility", *Church Life Journal*, July 24, 2018, https://churchlifejournal.nd.edu/articles/humanae-vitae-in-light-of-the-war-against-female-fertility/#_edn48.

and pleasure-making, having a sex change seems feasible. Elaborate surgical and hormonal interventions can alter the appearance of the body and mimic sex markers, and that is enough for us now, because that is what bodily sex has become. A surgeon can make a "vagina" out of a wound, because the vagina is no longer seen as the door to a womb.

By the mid-twentieth century, "sex" *qua* biological sex was dethroned, both linguistically and conceptually. The word "sex" no longer served merely as shorthand for one's biological sexual identity, but expanded to indicate any kind of erotic genital activity. "Sexuality" no longer referred to one's maleness or femaleness, but to the flavor and expression of one's erotic desires. This dethroning of "sex" created a conceptual vacuum, one quickly filled by the term "gender".

The Rise of Gender

In the 1950s, the phrase "gender role" first appeared on the scene, thanks to its coinage by psychologist John Money.[3] Money, whose work is now considered controversial, to put it mildly, was one of the first prominent advocates of a *tabula rasa* view of the human person. Biological sex, he argued, does not have an intrinsic connection to men and women's social roles and behaviors. He drew a distinction between sex, a mere biological fact, and "gender"—a social identity that is a product of culture rather than nature.

John Money's most famous patient was David Reimer, who was brought to him as a baby after his penis was disfigured during a botched circumcision. Money, who believed that gender was entirely socially constructed,

---

[3] John Money et al., "An Examination of Some Basic Sexual Concepts: The Evidence of Human Hermaphroditism", *Bulletin of Johns Hopkins Hospital* 97, no. 4 (1955): 301–19.

convinced David's parents to raise him as a girl and entrust him to Money's clinical supervision. David happened to be an identical twin, and Money saw a golden opportunity to run a controlled experiment to test his theories. David's parents unfortunately agreed, subjecting him to more genital surgeries and renaming him Brenda.

As part of his ongoing experiment, Money met with the twins annually throughout their childhood. His sessions with them were disturbing and invasive, involving clear instances of sexual abuse, such as compelling the two children to enact various sexual positions and inspect one another's genitalia.[4] As a teenager, David became suicidal and rejected his female identity, eventually learning the truth about his sex from his parents. He underwent more surgeries in an attempt to reverse the forced reassignment and took the name David (his birth name was Bruce). As an adult, David got married and adopted three children, and for a time, it seemed like he might be able to reclaim a normal life for himself—until May 4, 2004, when David took his own life at the age of thirty-eight, just two years after his twin brother's own suicide.

Money's attempt to demonstrate the veracity of his theories failed catastrophically; his theories proved to be not only erroneous, but *fatal* for his two research subjects. Unfortunately, this tragedy took decades to play out, and in the meantime, Money's malleable and disembodied concept of gender swept through the academy, becoming thoroughly entrenched in feminist theory and the social sciences.

Thanks to Money's innovations, this newly conceived idea of gender as distinct from sex became a site of resistance to essentialism, which was viewed in resolutely

[4] John Colapinto, *As Nature Made Him: The Boy Who Was Raised as a Girl*, 2nd ed. (New York: Harper Perennial, 2006).

negative terms. Supplanting the earlier paradigm, which relied on the holistic category of sex to classify men and women, a new paradigm emerged that distinguished between sex as a basic, biological reality and gender as a collection of socially constructed norms and ideals that are associated with each sex and mistakenly read as natural. This is the classic, second-wave feminist understanding of sex and gender, the one I inherited when I began my feminist studies. Sex refers to biology, and gender refers to the social meanings attached to sex.

We can understand why this distinction appealed to feminists, because it facilitated an important move beyond reductive and often misogynistic definitions of what it means to be a woman. Historically, arguments appealing to "natural" weaknesses or deficiencies in women have been used to justify denying them certain rights and opportunities, such as the right to vote or attend medical school. At times, differences between the sexes have been understood as differences in value and translated into rigid, sex-specific roles, creating a hierarchy of superiority and inferiority in favor of men. Without the concept of gender as distinct from sex, such ideas about woman are easily naturalized and seen as innate and inevitable rather than as distortions of culture. Let's look at some of these arguments in very basic terms:

Premise 1: Men and women are essentially or ontologically different.

Premise 2: Every difference represents a difference in value.

Conclusion: Men are essentially superior to women.

Premise 1: Men and women are essentially or ontologically different.

Premise 2:   These differences can be easily summa-
              rized in a list of contrasting traits that char-
              acterize each sex (for example, women are
              inherently more emotional, while men
              are inherently more rational).

Conclusion: The differences between men and women
              are clearly defined and necessitate distinct,
              sex-specific roles in the home and society.

In an attempt to overturn the conclusions of female inferiority and rigid sex roles, feminists rejected the first premise
of each argument, rallying their forces against essentialism.
Gender became the primary conceptual tool for dislodging
the idea that men and women are two essentially different
kinds of human beings.

At first glance, the distinction between sex and gender in this initial feminist usage seems straightforward:
sex is a basic fact referring to one's biology (femaleness or
maleness), and gender refers to the collection of cultural
meanings associated with each sex. Upon further examination, however, it becomes difficult to understand where
the demarcation between the two actually lies. Take the
notion that women are more nurturing, for example. Is
this idea a product of biology or culture?

The underlying problem, of course, is that humans are
both social and biological beings; our neuroplastic brains
respond to our environment, and our biological abilities
and limits shape cultural norms. We are formed through
an ongoing and ultimately mysterious interplay between
nature and nurture. Neatly distinguishing between sex
and gender, then, oversimplifies the complexity of human
personhood.

One can easily see, however, why gender was adopted
as a helpful tool in advocating for women's rights. It added

some much-needed nuance to the age-old "woman question", enabling feminists to argue that some sex-specific norms spring from culture rather than nature, and therefore cultural changes were necessary to give women greater social equality. (It should be noted, however, that first-wave feminists successfully won legal rights for women *without* the help of "gender".)

Are there costs that accompany these supposed benefits? How does introducing gender as a lens through which we understand ourselves subtly alter our conception of the human person? Once gender entered the theoretical scene, it quickly became the dominant force. The precarious, see-saw balance that feminist theory tried to maintain between sex and gender was eventually lost; in the postmodern turn of the third wave, the distinction between them grew into an outright schism. Sex retracted in its sphere of influence, becoming a discrete set of markers on an objectified body that carries little or no intrinsic meaning.

Ultimately, the concept of gender has driven a wedge between *body* and *identity*. Sex once referred to a bodily given, a fact of nature. In gender-world, the power of the body to constitute identity is diminished. "Woman" no longer refers simply to one's sex, but rather to one's gender, which has become an amorphous cultural construction that has a tenuous relationship to bodily sex. Once this distance between bodily sex and identity was enabled via gender, it did not take long—merely a few decades—for gender to shift meanings once again, becoming entirely disconnected from sex, which has paved the way for an even more fragmented and unstable understanding of personhood. Because gender is no longer anchored in bodily realities, it has become a postmodern juggernaut, impossible to capture, impossible to name. Unlike sex, "gender" can be continually altered and redeployed, and we are witnessing in real time the wild proliferation of its meaning.

Genderwocky

Pop narratives about gender often speak as if gender is something *real*, even though the concept itself resists the slightest hint of realism—or consistency. *Gender is a spectrum! Gender is fluid! Gender is innate! Gender is in the brain! Gender is a construct!* While the emphatic rhetoric suggests that the truth of gender is at last being unveiled, it is increasingly difficult to settle on a definition of gender at all, because there are multiple and often contradictory definitions on offer. Let's take a brief and nonexhaustive tour.

First, there is the decidedly "un-woke" definition that sees gender as a simple synonym for biological sex. This is the view of the uninitiated man-on-the-street, who checks the M box on a form without dwelling on the question.

Then there is the second-wave feminist definition that defines gender as the social and cultural *accoutrements* of each sex. Once cutting-edge, this definition is becoming outmoded, although still prevalent among feminists of a certain age.

A further iteration is the now-classic one offered by Judith Butler, godmother of gender theory. Butler, remember, argues that gender is an unconscious and socially compelled performance, a series of acts and behaviors that create the illusion of an essential identity of "man" and "woman". In this view, gender is *entirely* a social construct, a complex fiction that we inherit and then repeatedly reenact.

One can find yet *another* definition in a common transgender narrative: gender as the sex of the soul, the innate manhood or womanhood that may or may not "align" with the sex of the body. In this understanding, gender is decidedly *not* a mere construct, but is rather a pre-social reality, the inner truth against which the body must be measured.

Even more recently we have the cute and overly complicated understanding of gender popularized by the "Gender Unicorn" and "Genderbread Person" memes (the latter of which has already undergone four separate revisions in its brief existence). In this model, personal identity is collated from a menu of attributes, each of which runs along a spectrum. *Gender identity*, à la the trans definition above, is located in the mind: "how you, in your head, experience and define your gender". *Gender expression*, a trickle-down version of Butlerian performativity, refers to one's external appearance and acts: "how you present gender". *Sex*, which is "assigned" rather than recognized at birth, is confined between the legs. Rounding out the list is *attraction*, which is further parsed into two subcategories: physical and emotional.[5]

My students and I once mapped out these definitions on the board, lining them up for a side-by-side comparison. Rather than a row of neat little ducks, we found ourselves with a gaggle of mythical creatures that looked nothing alike. Several of these definitions, employed regularly by genderists, are contradictory, even mutually exclusive. If gender is completely a social construct, how can it also be innate and unchangeable?

Moreover, when used by activists, the term "gender" is defined in a circular and self-referential way. Take, for

---

[5] "Genderbread Person v4.0", Genderbread Person, last accessed September 3, 2021, https://www.genderbread.org/wp-content/uploads/2018/10/Genderbread-Person-v4-Poster.png.

example, the terms in a "Trans Glossary" featured on the University of Oregon's HR website. "Gender identity" is defined as "a person's sense of their own gender".[6] Yet there is no entry for "gender". The glossary includes definitions of "gender expression" and "gender role" that similarly refer back to the concept of gender without defining it.

My recent HR compliance training—the one that unsuccessfully tried to get me to use the phrase "pregnant person"—performed similar gymnastics. First, the training stated that "the terms 'sex' and 'gender' are often used interchangeably" and we need to go into more detail to understand each term. Fair enough. *However*, the next paragraph literally conflated the two terms with a slash, asserting that one's "assigned sex/gender" might conflict with one's "gender identity". Again, the word "gender" itself was never defined.

There is rhetorical sleight-of-hand at work here. The reader is first put off balance, subtly led to believe that she is not using the terms "sex" and "gender" correctly. After sowing these seeds of doubt, the training proceeds by using those very terms without clearly defining them, keeping them malleable, open to various meanings, which the reader readily accepts, assuming any lack of clarity must be due to her own ignorance.

It's difficult to know whether this is an explicit strategy or simply the product of unclear and faddish thinking. I'm not sure which option is more depressing: the idea that this radical revision of identity is a runaway train, barreling down the track because the gears of basic logic have broken

---

[6] "Trans Glossary 101", University of Oregon Human Resources, https://hr.uoregon.edu/hr-programs-services/work-life-resources/navigating-work-and-life/gender-identity-expression-and-0.

down, or that these contortions of word and thought are strategic moves. My suspicion is that both are true.

One can see more circularity in the increasingly common classification of woman as someone (anyone!) who identifies as a woman. This looping definition sends me right down a rabbit hole and into a frustratingly nonsensical conversation with a giant smoking caterpillar who sneers down at me from atop a large mushroom.

"What, pray, are *you*?" asks the caterpillar.

"I'm a woman."

"Oh *are* you?"

"Yes, at least ..." I pause, suddenly unsure. "I think so?"

"Do you *feel* like a woman?"

"I'm not sure", I say. "What does it mean to feel like a woman?"

"To feel like a woman is to be a woman", pronounces the caterpillar, taking a long drag from his hookah.

"But what is a woman?"

"Someone who feels like a woman."

"But ... what does it mean to feel like a woman, if being a woman is defined as feeling like a woman?"

"Transphobe", puffs the caterpillar.

That's me, a dizzy little Alice, smoke rings spinning round my head. Not phobic at all, but oh so curious and curiouser. What *is* this thing called gender? If the word is an egg, and I crack it open, what will I find inside? The more I study what gender has become, the more it feels like an empty signifier, a word that is only a shell, conveniently waiting to be filled with whatever meaning is most useful.

How many possibilities there are! There is a gender category for every proclivity, every flicker of mood, every possible aesthetic. Not sure if you feel like a man or woman? No problem. There are infinite options. Here is a small sampling from the ever-growing menu:

- *Agender*: a person without gender[7]
- *Bigender*: having two genders; exhibiting cultural characteristics of male and female roles[8]
- *Trigender*: This is a gender identity term that most often means one of two things. First, a trigender person may feel as though they are not man or woman, but are also not in between those two labels. As such, a trigender person defines their gender identity in a third category, which is not situated in between man/woman. Second, trigender can also mean a person who feels that they are a blending of three gender identities.[9]

If this *eins, zwei, drei* approach isn't your style, you can also work with fractions:

- *Demigender*: A person who feels partially, but not completely, connected to a particular gender identity.
- *Demifluid*: A person whose gender identity is partially fluid whilst the other part(s) are static.
- *Demiflux*: A person whose gender identity is partially fluid, with the other part(s) being static. This differs from demifluid as flux indicates that one of the genders is nonbinary.[10]

[7] University of Oregon, "Trans Glossary".

[8] Student Affairs, "LGBTQ Glossary", Johns Hopkins University, last accessed October 5, 2021, https://studentaffairs.jhu.edu/lgbtq/education/glossary/.

[9] Gender and Sexuality Center, "Trans* Identities and Lives Glossary", University of Rhode Island, last accessed October 5, 2021, https://web.uri.edu/gender-sexuality/resources/lgbtqa-glossary/trans-101-glossary/.

[10] University of Kent, "Trans Student Support Policy", last updated February 2, 2018, https://www.kent.ac.uk/studentservices/files/Trans%20Student%20Support%20Policy%2020%20Feb%202018.pdf.

With so many options, it's easy to get decision fatigue. In this situation, you can go big, and I mean *way* big—as in, beyond the boundaries of space and time.

- *Pangender*: refers to a gender identity whereby a person identifies with a multitude, and perhaps infinite (going beyond the current knowledge of genders) number of genders either simultaneously, to varying degrees, or over the course of time.[11]

These are not terms culled from random blogs and discussion forums. These are all taken, verbatim, from official websites of American and British universities. While it might be tempting to eye-roll and hand-wave away what those "crazy college kids" are doing, I would make this reply: official websites are run by administrators, not students, and what happens on campus quickly makes its way into the broader culture, corporate sector, public sphere, and education system as a whole. These students will graduate, after all, and enter the workforce. It's clear from the HR training I just completed that this is already happening.

Feeling Like a Woman

All of these definitions of gender are based on a subjective sense of identification, on how one "feels". But what does it mean to "feel" like a man or a woman or neither? Let's approach this question by way of an analogy, heading into a territory where the lines between categories have not yet been blurred. If I say that I "feel" like I'm a cat or that I "identify with" being a cat, I'm expressing that I have an

---

[11] "Trans Inclusion Guidance", University of Essex, August 2018, archived at https://web.archive.org/web/20210127015819/https://www.essex.ac.uk/-/media/documents/study/outreach/transgender-guidance.pdf.

affinity with what I imagine it must be like to be a cat. I cannot have direct, firsthand knowledge of what it is *actually* like to be a cat, because I am human, not feline.

To bring the analogy even closer, within the realm of the same species—let's say that I have a strong affinity with Italians. I am American, by the objective fact of being born and raised in America, but perhaps I nonetheless "feel" more Italian than American. I love to eat pasta, to gesture emphatically with my hands; I'm Catholic. I even have an Italian last name, albeit through marriage. But because I'm not *actually* Italian, what I am identifying with is only my perception, my fantasy, of what it might be like to be Italian.

Let's make the analogy even more pointed and discomfiting. Let's say I tell you that I'm not really a white girl, even though that's what I look like. In truth, I'm a black girl trapped in a white girl's body. My brain is black, even though my body is white. I know this because I *feel* it. I hate my white skin and straight hair. I feel at home around black people; I love hip-hop and basketball and Toni Morrison. I don't like white culture. I feel like a misfit in a room full of white people. I have a black soul.

I hope that anyone reading the above paragraph has a strong and instinctive reaction that what I am saying is ridiculous. I hope it reads as laughable, even offensive. If I were to make those claims in sincerity, I would be swiftly tied to a stake and set aflame for the sin of cultural appropriation—by the same people who would celebrate me as a courageous hero if I came out as a man. The boundaries between races and cultures are more policed than ever, but the boundary between the sexes has become completely porous.

"To feel" is not "to be". A white girl *cannot* know what it is like to be a black girl. She can only know what a white girl *imagines* it must be like to be black. A man *cannot* know what it is like to be a woman. He can only imagine, from an outside perspective, what it might be like. When he claims to be a woman, he is identifying with a fantasy. And, too often, that fantasy is constructed from the flimsy chaff of stereotypes.

When I was in my first year of graduate school in gender studies, I remember watching a television special on transgender kids. This was 2007 or so, and I was living in the UK. Even in my secular academic circle, feminism had not yet become fully allied with the transgender narrative. The current transgender wave, particularly among adolescents, was still years away. This special was about a little boy who insisted he was a girl, and the parents had begun to raise him that way. He was probably seven or eight and had already adopted a new name and social identity as a girl. What struck me then, and sticks with me now, is the evidence of this boy's ostensible girlness: he loved the color pink, he preferred to play with dolls, and he liked to wear dresses. His room looked like a Pepto Bismol bottle had exploded. Even the way this little boy spoke about being a girl had everything to do with the accessories of stereotypical femininity. There was an odor of consumerism wafting about the whole thing—as if the products we want define what we are.

My feminist grad student self was dubious. I did not recognize this version of girlness, except perhaps from a commercial for Barbie dolls. Certainly not in my own childhood. I was never into pink. My room was painted blue. I played with dolls and stuffed animals, but I also loved making fake swords out of rulers and tin foil and building Star Trek phasers from Legos. I liked wearing dresses as part of pretend-play, when I could temporarily escape my time and place and become someone new. Mostly, I wanted to wear clothes that allowed me to run, to feel my legs churn underneath me, swift and powerful.

In terms of stereotypes, I was a mixed bag. The idea that a boy is actually a girl because he likes pink seemed to me then, and does still, to be a regressive and decidedly unfeminist notion, a throwback to cartoonish understandings of femininity and masculinity.

If girlness and boyness no longer reside in the body, there is no other ground for these concepts *except* stereotypes. Remember the definition for "bigender" above, from Johns Hopkins University? *Exhibiting cultural characteristics of male and female roles*. My first reaction to this is well, shoot, who is *not* bigender in twenty-first-century America? Am I bigender simply because I am a breadwinner (stereotypically male role) and a mom who does lots of laundry (stereotypical female role)? Is my husband bigender because he is a stay-at-home parent (female role) and mows our lawn (male role)? Why is my identity as a woman threatened or lessened simply because I, a complex human being, happen to reflect a variety of stars in the vast constellation of sex-associated tasks and traits? Don't these silly definitions of gender end up keeping those regressive stereotypes entrenched?

There is a profound irony here. Through the vehicle of feminist theory, the concept of gender has displaced manhood and womanhood from bodily sex. Now, unmoored from the body altogether, gender is defined by the very cultural stereotypes that feminism sought to undo. In other words, when a girl recognizes that she does not fit the stereotypes of girlhood, she is now invited to question her sex rather than the stereotype.

The Age of Pygmalion

When gender remains rooted in sex—when womanhood refers to femaleness rather than the embodiment of a feminine stereotype—this allows "woman" to be a much roomier box, to encompass a diverse range of traits, roles, and body types. The box based on stereotypes is much narrower, confining womanhood to an artificial, airbrushed, hyped-up caricature that would exclude most human females, myself included.

When I go to Mass at my local parish, a situation that gathers together a diverse group of people, all ages and sizes, I do not see a single female who looks anything like Caitlyn Jenner on the cover of *Vanity Fair*. I see girls in sweatpants and sneakers, girls in lace veils and heels; I see tall women, short women, fat women, broad-shouldered women, thin women, huge- and small-breasted women, women with long hair, women with cropped hair, women in skirts, women in men's flannel shirts, women with wide hips, women with trim hips, women with rolls of soft flesh, women with wrinkles, sharp angles, concave chests. This assembly of the ordinary—this slice-of-life sample—looks nothing like the artifice displayed on magazine covers and billboards and the filtered reel of Instagram.

We are living in the Age of Pygmalion, that master artist from Ovid's *Metamorphoses* who wants a wife but despises real women. He picks up his hammer and chisel and constructs his ideal out of stone. He lusts after her; his image of woman is more desirable than the reality. In the original myth, Pygmalion wants to marry her, to bring her to his bed; in our time, Pygmalion wants to *be* her. Instead of a sculptor's tools, he works with scalpel and syringe. Instead of stone, he carves his fantasy into his own flesh.

In Ovid's tale, Pygmalion's creation comes alive through divine intervention, an on-high blast from the goddess Aphrodite. In our time, there are no capricious gods who can make fantasy seem real. There is only the power of language.

The University of Edinburgh's policy on trans equality gives the following directives for interacting with transgender people: "Think of the person as being the gender that they want you to think of them as", and "use the name and pronoun that the person asks you to."[12] These guidelines unwittingly make a startling concession: you have to actively *convince yourself* that this person's gender proclamation is true. Accepting that a man is really a woman and vice versa requires effort, a conscious exertion of thought, because this cuts against biology and common sense. Since the gender paradigm is not based on concrete reality, perpetuating this framework requires careful policing of thought and language.

This explains the intense focus on pronouns by today's activists. One *must* use the pronouns of the declared gender. Failure to do so is considered a malicious attack on a person's identity and dignity. Beyond mere offense, "misgendering" someone by using the incorrect pronouns is considered harmful, an act of violence.

I remember in high school being teased for having "man legs" and a moustache. This was deeply hurtful, of course, and it preyed upon my insecurities about how I looked as a young woman, that I was failing to live up to an ideal. It did not threaten the core of my identity as a woman, because I considered that to be a fact that I couldn't escape, whether I liked it or not. Today's concept of gender identity, however, is not based in material reality. A man who claims to be a woman is a woman in language only. For the postmodernist, that's enough, because *all* of reality, all of what we consider "true", is linguistically constructed.[13]

---

[12] "Trans Equality Policy", University of Edinburgh, last updated June 2016, http://www.docs.csg.ed.ac.uk/EqualityDiversity/Trans_Equality_Policy.pdf.

[13] This understanding of reality as constructed by language is shared by the most prominent postmodern theorists, such as Lyotard, Derrida, Foucault, and Barthes. See Christopher Butler, *Postmodernism: A Very Short Introduction* (Oxford: Oxford University Press, 2002), 21.

This means that the construct of gender identity must be continually buttressed by language in order to appear true. This requires not only a self-declaration of gender, but a declaration that is echoed by everyone else. If gender identity only exists in language, our language must be manipulated, or else the whole thing falls apart. That is what's at stake in the battle over pronouns: our understanding of reality itself.

The linguistic reshaping of reality is working its way into the law. The Equality Act is a bill under proposal in the United States as of 2021; it passed the House in 2019. This bill would amend the Civil Rights Acts of 1964, replacing the word "sex" with the three-headed Hydra of "sex (including sexual orientation and gender identity)". As always, gender identity is defined in a circular way, as "the gender-related identity, appearance, mannerisms, or other gender-related characteristics of an individual, regardless of the individual's sex at birth."[14] Legally redefining sex as something that includes gender identity, while in the same breath defining gender identity as something not necessarily related to sex, is nonsensical. This linguistic contortion attempts to hold together two things that are in direct contradiction: the view that gender is based in sex and the view that gender is *not* based in sex. Moreover, this definition establishes gender—manhood and womanhood—to be a matter of appearance and stereotypes rather than biology.

Let me state emphatically that I have no objection to legally protecting all American citizens from unjust discrimination. The problem arises when sex-based rights and protections are eroded to accommodate the novel and inherently unstable concept of gender identity. This bill

[14] H.R. 5, 117th Cong. (2021–2022).

would effectively outlaw sex-segregated spaces, programs, institutions. This bill would end women's sports as we know it, because, no matter how they identify, biological men have an undeniable physical advantage. Spaces such as women's locker rooms, bathrooms, prisons, and domestic shelters would no longer be limited to females only. Spaces like these can only be preserved through maintaining boundaries, boundaries that respect material reality, that acknowledge the fundamental fact that women and men are biologically distinct. Sex-segregated spaces, by and large, do not exist for the benefit of men, except to protect the worst among them from their darkest impulses. These boundaries exist to protect women and girls, a population that is more vulnerable to sexual exploitation and violence.

I do not make this argument solely out of fear, fear that the erasure of clear boundaries will put women and girls at risk. I am also appealing to beauty: the quiet beauty of being a female body in a room alone with other female bodies.

I traveled to Israel in 2019, and when we were staying on the shores of Galilee, my husband and I walked to the beach together, hoping to dip our limbs into the same waters where Jesus fished. As we stood on the shore together, a man wearing a yarmulke came over and told us, in a polite and matter-of-fact way, that this beach was for men only; there was a women-only beach just over the rise. I was surprised, a little embarrassed, but thanked him and walked around to the women's area, disrobing down to my suit and diving into the sea. After a while, a number of my female students joined, as well as some Israeli women and girls, and we all swam and splashed around, in collective female solitude. Some of my students bristled at the segregation, seeing it as sexist. I found it refreshing. We weren't *doing* anything consciously feminine, as too often happens at women's retreats and conferences, which I tend to dread. This was a space set aside just for existing as women. As I floated in the Sea of Galilee, feeling the fish flicker and dash beneath me, I experienced the hush of freedom—the bliss of being, for the moment, unobserved.

There is something sacred about these female-only spaces, even the swampy women's locker room at the local pool. This is perhaps the only place where girls are able to see the unsung beauty of female nudity that is not at all sexualized, to witness firsthand the diversity of the female form, to have a concrete image that can contradict the harmful fictions displayed everywhere else: to see breasts that droop, flesh that sags, pubic hair that hangs; to see an old lady perfunctorily washing between her rolls in the shower, unselfconsciously caring for the aging body she belongs to, the body she has always been.

Artifice

I have three stories to tell: two myths and a difficult truth.

The first myth is a sixth-century Sanskrit *jataka*, a tale recounting a previous life of the Buddha. In this story, a bodhisattva named Rūpyāvatī cuts off her own breasts to feed a starving mother who is about to eat her newborn child out of desperation. Rūpyāvatī is praised for this radical act of self-sacrifice, and in recompense her breasts are divinely restored. Thus far, this story is viscerally beautiful and sharply affirming of the feminine: a woman saving another woman from death through the gift of her own life-giving flesh. Life and death edge close together here, almost blurring into one another—the new mother is on the brink of killing that to which she just gave life—until Rūpyāvatī intervenes, and the specter of death is driven away by a gesture of self-giving love.

The story does not end there. After Rūpyāvatī's female body is restored to wholeness, she makes a request to "the lord of the gods" to be freed from it altogether:

> "O brahmin, by means of this truth of mine,
> Let my sex become male immediately,
> For manhood is an abode of virtue in this world."
>
> As soon as she had spoken these words,
> She attained the state of a man....
>
> And when her two breasts—
> Swollen like the frontal lobes of an elephant in rut

Saw just a few beard hairs as dark as collyrium powder
Appearing on that moon-like face,
They immediately disappeared into a broad chest
As if out of shame.[1]

This is a bewildering reversal. Why were her breasts
restored to wholeness in the first place, only to be banished
again just a page later? A story that seemed to exhibit regard
for the female body is suddenly turncoat, sending this clear
message: it is better to have a healed female body than a
maimed one, but it is better still to become male altogether.

I had a similar reading experience with the story of Caenis
in Ovid's *Metamorphoses*. Caenis, "famed for her beauty",
resistant to marriage, is raped by the god Neptune as she
is "walking/on a lonely shore". This was apparently such
an enjoyable experience for Neptune that he, like some
sadistic genie, offers to grant her one wish in recompense:

And Caenis answered,

"The wrong you've done demands the great prayer
That I never be able to suffer this again. Make me
A woman no longer and you will have given me all."

She spoke the last words in a huskier voice
That seemed like a man's. And so it was,
For the sea god had already answered her prayer....[2]

Both women, when given the chance, ask to be made into
men by divine intervention—one to achieve a loftier state
of being; the other to be made invulnerable to rape.

There is a sense in which these myths are coming true in
our time. In the past two years, there has been an exponential

[1] Daniel Lopez, ed., *Buddhist Scriptures* (New York: Penguin, 2004), 168.
[2] Ovid, *Metamorphoses*, trans. Stanley Lombardo (Indianapolis: Hackett, 2010), 331–32.

rise of patients presenting at gender clinics desiring transition, as well as a major demographic shift. Prior to the internet era, those seeking transition were typically natal males in their forties. In 2014, this began to change dramatically. By 2019, three times as many natal females were seeking transition, and most of them teenagers.

Gender dysphoria, the current clinical term of art, refers to the extreme psychological distress that stems from a feeling of incongruence with one's sex. Gender dysphoria among children and adolescents used to be exceptionally rare, affecting only 0.1% of kids, and those almost entirely boys.[3] Prior to 2012, there is no scientific evidence of adolescent girls experiencing gender dysphoria at all.[4] What we are witnessing is a novel phenomenon.

The Gender Identity Development Service (GIDS) in the UK provides a clear source of data for this trend; their figures give a snapshot of a phenomenon that is occurring across Europe, the United States, and Canada. Let's look at the data on child and adolescent gender referrals specifically, where transition rates are skyrocketing. In 2010, 138 patients were referred for gender treatment. In 2015, the number jumped to 1,409 and continued to climb steadily, reaching 2,748 referrals in the latest year on record, 2019–2020. In less than a decade, gender referrals had increased by almost 2,000%.[5]

While there has been a spike in referrals for boys, the rise in female referrals outpaces this by a factor of three. This disparity is most pronounced between the ages of 11 and 17. For example, of the almost 500 14-year-olds referred

---

[3] Abigail Shrier, *Irreversible Damage: The Transgender Craze Seducing Our Daughters* (Washington, D.C.: Regnery, 2020), xxi.

[4] Shrier, *Irreversible Damage*, xxi.

[5] "Referrals to GIDS, Financial Years 2015–16 to 2019–20", NHS Gender Identity Service, last accessed October 18, 2021, https://gids.nhs.uk/number -referrals. These figures are regularly updated by GIDS and subject to change.

to GIDS in 2019–2020, over 400 were girls. Overall, 75% of adolescent referrals that year were for natal females.

This new wave of trans-identification among young people differs from earlier "classic" presentations of what used to be called transsexualism. Ray Blanchard, a prominent psychiatrist and sexologist, created a basic typology for transsexuals in the late 1980s, categorizing them into two main groups. The first group, "androphilic transsexuals", are boys who are more stereotypically feminine in behavior and appearance and grow up to be homosexual. The second group, "autogynephilic transsexuals", are men who are sexually aroused by the thought of being a woman; these men are often heterosexual and typically transition later in life.[6] Blanchard's work has become highly controversial because it looks at transgenderism as a clinical problem, rather than a political identity. His taxonomy is still relevant for men who fall into those classic categories, but it does not explain the rapid explosion of emergent gender identities among young people, especially young women.

This is a complex phenomenon, influenced by multiple factors, several of which I will trace throughout this chapter. The most significant factor, however, is the development of the gender paradigm itself. This has produced a "looping effect", wherein certain human experiences are categorized and interpreted through the framework of gender theory, which in turn shapes those experiences and reinforces the framework.[7] A man with autogynephilia, a woman with a history of sex abuse who hates

---

[6] Louise Perry, "What Is Autogynephilia? An Interview with Ray Blanchard", *Quillette*, November 6, 2019, https://quillette.com/2019/11/06/what-is-autogynephilia-an-interview-with-dr-ray-blanchard/.

[7] For more on the looping effect in relation to gender, see Mark Yarhouse and Julia Sadusky, *Emerging Gender Identities: Understanding the Diverse Experiences of Today's Youth* (Ada, MI: Brazos Press, 2020).

her body, an autistic kid who feels different from everyone around him, a lonely teenager desperate for community and identity—any one of these people, or all of them, might find in the gender paradigm an explanation for their pain (*you must be trans*), and a deceptively simple solution (*change your gender, and you will finally be whole*).

I do not think that dismantling the framework of gender theory will make the experience of sexual incongruence magically disappear. There will still be individuals who have that experience, whether it's caused by a neurological condition or trauma or simply having a personality that is out of step with cultural sex stereotypes. What I am concerned with here, and throughout this book, is questioning the framework our culture has built to interpret and categorize those experiences—a framework that, by the way, was not developed by trans-identifying people. The truth, I believe, is the inverse: *the development of that framework has led to transgender identification.* There are people in turmoil, and the gender paradigm has become the dominant lens for interpreting that turmoil, and that's not good.

Here is the difficult truth: we are living in an era when our young women are increasingly deciding they would be better off as men. For Caenis and Rūpyāvatī, as for many young women in our time, femaleness has become an unbearable burden rather than a gift.

And this should alarm us.

Hypersexualization

What is fueling the flight from womanhood? I've been watching this trend unfold from afar for several years, trying to track its genesis. I'm often reminded of a text I used to teach in gender theory: "The Body and the Reproduction of Femininity", by feminist theorist Susan Bordo. Bordo is writing from a postmodern feminist perspective, drawing from Foucault's ideas about social forces having influence over the body. While I reject postmodernism as a totalizing worldview, there are some insights we can glean from postmodern philosophy, such as how language and society shape our perceptions of reality and identity. Bordo's analysis of widespread anorexia and bulimia in the 1970–1980s can perhaps shed some light on this new epidemic of our time.

According to Bordo, the body is a "medium of culture", a "surface on which the central rules, hierarchies, and even metaphysical commitments of a culture are inscribed and thus reinforced through the concrete language of the body."[8] Bordo argues that certain pathologies arise in response to the gendered ideals of particular eras. For example, she draws a correlation between Victorian ideals of delicate, passive femininity and the rise of feminine hysteria in that period and a similar parallel between the 1950s housewife ideal and a corresponding increase in agoraphobia in the adjacent decades. In each of these examples, she writes, "we find the body of the sufferer deeply inscribed with an ideological construction of femininity emblematic of the periods in question." Eating disorders, Bordo argues, function similarly, as an exaggerated display of cultural ideals of womanhood, as well as a rebellion against them, "a species of unconscious feminist protest". As part of her analysis, Bordo quotes from Aimee Liu's memoir of anorexia:

> At school, she discovers that her steadily shrinking body is admired, not so much as an aesthetic or sexual object but

---

[8] Susan Bordo, "The Body and the Reproduction of Femininity: A Feminist Appropriation of Foucault", in *Gender, Body, Knowledge*, ed. Alison M. Jaggar (New Brunswick, NJ: Rutgers University Press, 1989), 13.

for the strength of will and self-control it projects.... As her body begins to lose its traditional feminine curves, its breasts and hips and rounded stomach, and begins to feel and look more like a spare, lanky male body, she begins to feel untouchable, out of reach of hurt, "invulnerable, clean and hard as the bones etched into my silhouette," as one woman described it. She despises, in particular, all those parts of her body that continue to mark her as female. "If only I could eliminate [my breasts]," says Liu, "cut them off if need be."[9]

The parallels between this experiential description of anorexia and gender dysphoria are striking. Liu does not simply want to rid her body of fat; she wants to erase her femaleness, to have the curves that mark her as a woman shrivel up and disappear.

I'm not the only one who has noted parallels between body-image dysphoria and gender dysphoria. Lisa Littman, a researcher at Brown University who published a recent study on "rapid onset gender dysphoria" among teenage girls, describes finding "many potential parallels between anorexia nervosa and gender dysphoria" in the course of her research.[10] In appealing to Bordo's analysis of anorexia, I'm not proposing a totalizing theory that explains all instances of gender dysphoria. I am arguing that one dimension of this broader cultural phenomenon is a rebellion, a protest, against the hypersexualization of the female body.

It is difficult, maybe impossible, to grow up female and not absorb the painful idea behind the myth of Caenis:

[9] Bordo, "The Body", 23.
[10] Jonathan Kay, "An Interview with Lisa Littman, Who Coined the Term 'Rapid Onset Gender Dysphoria'", *Quillette*, March 19, 2019, https://quillette .com/2019/03/19/an-interview-with-lisa-littman-who-coined-the-term -rapid-onset-gender-dysphoria/.

to be a woman is to be vulnerable, particularly to sexual exploitation. The idea that women exist primarily for the pleasure of men has never been more explicit, more omnipresent, than in our ostensibly feminist age. Some feminists have even embraced this, singing the sex-positive praises of pornography and prostitution as somehow liberating for women. Even those willing to name and criticize the pervasive sexualization of women and girls are less willing to acknowledge the ways in which feminism itself has contributed to it. I find it maddening to watch avowed feminists decry the rotten fruits of the sexual revolution while they simultaneously tend its roots.

This hypersexualization of femaleness becomes, for some trans-identified men, a kind of sexual fetish: a simultaneous fetishization of the female body as well as their own bodies. They define woman as a sex object and desire to be that sex object. In his memoir *Whipping Girl*, trans-identified male Julia Serano writes candidly about his own rape fantasies: "While I never really believed the cliché about women being good for only one thing, that sentiment kept creeping into my fantasies." He describes these fantasies, which began in adolescence, as "bastard Catholic sacraments"; he tried to purge himself of guilt "by combining my desire to be female with self-inflicted penance and punishment."[11] Another trans-identified man, Andrea Long Chu, writes that pornography is "the quintessential definition of femaleness".[12] To be female is to be dominated, to be subjected to another's desire, "to become what someone else wants."[13] Chu criticizes Blanchard's taxonomy because he thinks "autogynephilia" is not a

[11] Julia Serano, *Whipping Girl: A Transexual Woman on Sexism and the Scapegoating of Femininity* (New York: Basic Books, 2016), 274–75.

[12] Andrea Long Chu, *Females: A Concern* (New York: Verso, 2019), 63.

[13] Chu, *Females*, 74.

paraphilia, but characteristic of all human sexuality. Everyone is female, he says, and everyone hates it.

Several Catholic writers have picked up on the fact that Chu's writing exhibits dark parallels to the Christian spiritual ideal of surrendering to God, which is most perfectly expressed in Mary. As Angela Franks puts it, "Chu's worldview is an eroticized, photographic negative of Christianity, in which receptivity to God's loving action has been transformed into submission to the imperious dictates of desire."[14] In these nihilistic accounts, the personal and bodily reality of womanhood is erased, abstracted into masochistic desire, as if "female" is simply a Platonic form for sexual objectification.

When I read these accounts of femaleness, I feel like I want to hide; I want the visibly female features of my body to dissolve and disappear entirely. If this is what it means to be a woman—to be degraded, dominated, depersonalized, reduced to an object for someone else's use—then I want no part in it. *Make me a woman no longer.* Is it any wonder that our girls are in revolt?

Unfortunately, this mutiny is misdirected. These young women are rebelling, understandably, against the hypersexualization of the female body, but in doing so, they are turning against the body itself. To quote Bordo once more, "although we may talk meaningfully of protest, then, I would emphasize the counterproductive, tragically self-defeating (indeed self-deconstructing) nature of

[14] Angela Franks, "Andrea Long Chu Says You Are a Female, and He's Only Partly Wrong", *Public Discourse*, December 10, 2019, https://www.thepublicdiscourse.com/2019/12/58719/. See also Eve Tushnet, "Is Everyone Female?", *Commonweal*, February 7, 2020, https://www.commonwealmagazine.org/everyone-female. Also Stephen Abudato, "Andrea Long Chu's *Females* Subverts Subversiveness", *Catholic World Report*, Sept 16, 2020, https://www.catholicworldreport.com/2020/09/16/andrea-long-chus-females-subverts-subversiveness/.

that protest."[15] While Bordo is writing here of anorexia, I would apply this statement to the current epidemic of gender transition. Shedding the visible markers of femaleness may feel as empowering for the transgender teen as it does for the anorexic, but these forms of protest are ultimately violent and self-destructive. The better rebellion, and the more difficult one, is learning to see one's beauty and dignity as a woman amidst a culture that denies it.

The female body, in our shared imagination, no longer signals creation, nourishment, and primal compassion, but rather the prospect of sterile pleasure. Our bodies are tools for gratification. That's what becoming a woman felt like—like I was being seen as less than a whole human being and more as an instrument of sexual pleasure.

Because of this, I've never liked having breasts. They appeared far too early, for one thing. In sixth grade, I was a monster, a head taller than everyone else and already in a C-cup; the boys in my class made up a clever jingle about my breast size. I was greatly relieved when, in seventh grade, another unfortunate girl sprang into a D-cup, and I was no longer Queen of the Bust. My breasts made me feel exposed; the metamorphosis of my body felt like a betrayal. I wanted to retreat into flat-chested anonymity. I marveled at the girls who seemed to enjoy having breasts, who wanted to call attention to them, to puff them up and present them to the world like freshly baked loaves. I only ever wanted to hide them.

Predictably, growing a woman's body while still a teenager drew the attention of older males, and I was ushered into the complicated world of sex too soon. It was hard not to feel that my body, especially those breasts, those damned *protrusions*, were partly to blame for this initiation.

[15] Bordo, "The Body", 21.

There are many times, during those tumultuous years of emerging womanhood, when I would have readily prayed Rūpyāvatī's prayer, to have my breasts recede in shame and disappear.

That wasn't a live option for me. Maybe if it had been, I would have contemplated taking it. I was born twenty years too early. Don't misunderstand: I am voicing not regret, but relief. I am relieved that when I was in the throes of self-discovery in college, the only thing I had to question was my faith and my sexual orientation, not my femaleness itself. *That* was a given, and so I learned instead to live with breasts, rather than be rid of them. Because of this, I've had the gift of experiencing their *telos*: sources of life and sweet milk for my babies. My chronic dis-ease with having breasts, especially cumbersome lactating ones, is temporarily suspended in the wordless communion of breastfeeding. Even when I'm not lactating, even for the woman who *never* lactates, I now understand that breasts are visible signs of feminine self-gift, the capacity and call to nourish the souls and bodies—the full personhood—of those who come under our care.

Despite this knowledge, I will admit to feeling relief when weaning time comes and my breasts become inconspicuous again, withered and discreet.

Online Avatars

Over the course of writing this book, I've read and listened to dozens of stories from trans-identified women and girls, many of whom are "detransitioners", women who for a time identified as transgender men, often altering their bodies permanently, who then decided to return to identifying as women. The process of transition is a series of domino-steps that typically lead from one to the next: first, the linguistic change, choosing new pronouns and a new name; then, medical interventions, such as taking testosterone shots, amputating breasts, or undergoing cosmetic surgery on genitalia. Girls who go through a linguistic transition and then revert back are called "desisters", because they "desist" from the transition process before it is complete. Those who go through both linguistic and medical transition and then revert are called "detransitioners" or just "detrans".

Detrans stories are becoming more common, despite the efforts of trans activists to dismiss and silence those voices. While transition is lauded and celebrated as a feat of authentic self-actualization, detransitioners are derided as traitors to the cause. Detransitioners are mischaracterized by activists as self-deluded counterfeits, "cis women" who were never "true trans" to begin with, whose stories can thus be disregarded. Detrans stories are threatening to some, because they serve as a mirror, reflecting back a discomfiting reality that is at odds with the fantasy of seamless, painless self-invention.

There is no singular reason for deciding to transition or deciding to detransition. Every story I've heard, like every human being, is unique. Yet there are patterns that emerge, commonalities among the stories that signal multiple causal forces at work. One of these is the topic discussed above: the hypersexualization of girls and women. Again and again, I hear transitioned women name the discomfort of nearing puberty and suddenly receiving unwanted sexual attention from men. For many of these girls, womanhood seemed synonymous with sexual objectification. It's no wonder they wanted to take refuge in a masculine identity. I know this discomfort well; it is part of my own history. I know the feeling of wanting to dissociate from a rapidly changing body, wanting to burrow inside myself, like a turtle ducking inside its shell—a shell that was, to my horror, growing breasts.

This common adolescent experience is complicated by another key factor, one that differentiates my coming-of-age in the eighties and nineties from the girlhood of today: the expansive world of the internet, which now mediates most of our social interactions. Today, the internet is like Jonah's whale, a beast that has swallowed us whole. We live in its dark belly, our faces lit by our screens.

When I was twelve, this sea monster was more like a playful dolphin I interacted with from time to time. These were the dial-up days: make sure no one's on the landline, and then wait five excruciating minutes for the clunky computer to connect sluggishly to the internet. Once I was online, I didn't see a lot of images, just bright-colored words against white or black screens, lame fonts and graphics, no videos at all. There were no influencers on Instagram and YouTube. There were no smartphone cameras with flattering filters. I was in graduate school when I joined Facebook, which was still limited to university communities. I was already a professor, Ph.D. in hand, by the time I got my first smartphone. When I was a tortured, awkward, self-loathing teenager, social media and its endlessly scrolling fantasies did not yet exist. Thank God.

In *all* the transition stories I've heard, the internet played a key role. Even in the story of Laura Reynolds, a woman my age, who transitioned well before the current escalation and before the existence of social media. Even she first encountered the tantalizing prospect of changing her sex on an internet message board.[16] More recent detransitioners describe being immersed in the world of the internet, binging on YouTube videos and Tumblr blogs, obsessively

[16] "Renegotiating Womanhood: A Detrans Story, with Laura", interview by Benjamin A. Boyce, January 21, 2020, YouTube video, 1:15, https://www.youtube.com/watch?v=4DOUcpFxKKw.

following trans influencers for tips on getting hormones, binding breasts, and crafting a convincing narrative of life-long dysphoria to appease doctors and family members.

The pro-trans sphere bears a stark resemblance to the "pro-ana" and "pro-mia" sphere: online sites and communities that promote anorexia and bulimia as a lifestyle choice and give advice to followers on losing weight, suppressing hunger, and hiding evidence of disordered eating. These communities almost worship eating disorders, deifying them as goddesses Ana and Mia. They see their approach to eating and exercise not as pathological, but as empowering, a source of discipline and control. Both pro-ana and pro-trans groups promote self-harm as liberation, relying on peer support and pressure to motivate followers in their pursuit of the ideal body.

The world of the internet lends itself to movements like this for several reasons. First, there is the ability to connect with like-minded people from all over the world and form insular communities. In the pro-trans sphere, adult activists often encourage teenagers to transition, showering them with encouragement and affection—affection that at times can cross the line into sexual grooming.[17] Many of the detrans stories I've heard describe this environment as cult-like, characterized by pathological groupthink and ideological conformity, advocating isolation from friends and family who raise questions or concerns about transition.

The pro-trans and pro-ana groups also share this feature: a concerted effort violently to impose a fantasized ideal onto the material reality of the body. Online, it is easy to believe that the body does not matter. Bodies on the internet are no longer "real"; they are flattened into carefully

---

[17] See, for example, Benjamin Boyce, "Coercion and Abuse in the Gender ID Community with GNC-Centric", interview by Benjamin A. Boyce, March 14, 2019, YouTube video, 1:13, https://www.youtube.com/watch?v=QAMar22Sock.

curated two-dimensional images. Self-invention in the realm of the internet is limitless. Our online selves are avatars, unbounded by physical circumstances that become inescapable in the world offline. Online, sex is merely a label selected from a scroll-down list, an exterior façade. Sex becomes gender, a curated aesthetic completely severed from reproductive potentiality. In some ways, transition is an attempt to create a real-word filter of an idealized body that can be imposed upon the self. To *appear* is to *become*.

Fortunately, the medical community and society writ large do not consider anorexia and bulimia as something to be celebrated, which keeps a lid on the contagion and keeps open the possibility that people with eating disorders can pursue healing. This is not the case, however, with the bodily contortions required to support a trans identity. Medical transition is now embraced as the standard of care for those suffering from gender dysphoria, despite the lack of high-quality evidence to support this approach. In 2016, the Obama administration conducted an exhaustive review of all existing peer-reviewed research on surgical remedies for gender dysphoria in order to decide whether those procedures should be covered by Medicare. After reviewing the evidence, they elected not to issue a National Coverage Determination, because the clinical evidence for the efficacy of these treatments remains inconclusive.[18]

More recently, in 2020 *The American Journal of Psychiatry* issued a correction to a 2019 study that initially seemed to suggest that medical transition is beneficial to mental health. The original study, however, did not compare outcomes between dysphoric individuals who received surgeries and those who did not. When the researchers compared their

---

[18] "Decision Memo for Gender Dysphoria and Gender Reassignment Surgery", Centers for Medicare and Medicaid Services, last modified August 30, 2016, https://www.cms.gov/medicare-coverage-database/details/nca-decision-memo.aspx?NCAId=282&bc=ACAAAAAAQAAA&.

initial findings against this control group, the benefit disappeared: "the results demonstrated no advantage of surgery in relation to subsequent mood or anxiety disorder-related health care visits or prescriptions or hospitalizations following suicide attempts." This updated finding is stunning: these invasive, expensive, irreversible medical interventions being pushed by the medical industry *showed no benefit to mental health*.[19] (The study did not even assess physical health.)

This correction received little media attention, unlike the study's original findings, and medical organizations and practitioners continue to push the affirmation model. Rather than exploring, through psychotherapy, why a particular individual might hate his or her body, the recommendation is to essentialize that self-hatred into an innate identity and permanently alter the body.

Medicalizing the Body

Let me pause here and note that not all trans-identifying people are on board with the affirmative care model. Many readily acknowledge the biological realities of their natal sex and would prefer to live quietly, outside the glaring spotlight of the culture wars. Some, in fact, actively oppose the extremes of trans activism, particularly when it comes to the medicalization of children.

---

[19] "Correction to Bränström and Pachankis", *American Journal of Psychiatry* 177, no. 8 (August 2020): 734, https://doi.org/10.1176/appi.ajp.2020.1778 correction. Original study: R. Bränström and J. E. Pachankis, "Reduction in Mental Health Treatment Utilization among Transgender Individuals after Gender-Affirming Surgeries: A Total Population Study", *American Journal of Psychiatry* 177, no. 8 (August 2020): 727–34, https://doi.org/10.1176/appi.ajp .2019.19010080.

One such person is Scott Newgent. Scott is a trans activist, but not the kind of activist pushing transition as a cure-all for teens and children in psychological distress. Scott advocates *for* the well-being of children, pushing back against the extremes of the gender paradigm. As part of this advocacy, Scott has written in graphic detail about the grueling (and in Scott's case, nearly fatal) process of medical transition:

> During my own transition, I had seven surgeries. I also had a massive pulmonary embolism, a helicopter life-flight ride, an emergency ambulance ride, a stress-induced heart attack, sepsis, a 17-month recurring infection due to using the wrong skin during a (failed) phalloplasty, 16 rounds of antibiotics, three weeks of daily IV antibiotics, the loss of all my hair, (only partially successful) arm reconstructive surgery, permanent lung and heart damage, a cut bladder, insomnia-induced hallucinations—oh and frequent loss of consciousness due to pain from the hair on the inside of my urethra. All this led to a form of PTSD that made me a prisoner in my apartment for a year. Between me and my insurance company, medical expenses exceeded $900,000.[20]

Scott is telling this story to counter the "gauzy rainbow" narrative of transition as safe, easy, painless—a magical treatment that can miraculously transform someone into the opposite sex. In reality, Scott emphasizes, one's appearance can change, but not one's sex. Even this cosmetic transformation can only be achieved at great cost to one's physical health.

[20] Scott Newgent, "Forget What Gender Activists Tell You. Here's What Medical Transition Looks Like", *Quillette*, October 6, 2020, https://quillette.com/2020/10/06/forget-what-gender-activists-tell-you-heres-what-medical-transition-looks-like/.

Scott's tireless activism is focused on protecting young people, who are increasingly swept up by a dangerous ideology—an ideology that is now fueling a billion-dollar industry. If Scott's surgical transition alone cost nearly one million dollars, just think how much money can be made putting thousands of people, including children and adolescents, on the path to a lifetime of medicalization. Medical transition, after all, is not a one-time event. Physical interventions, such as taking cross-sex hormones, must be continually maintained to prevent the reality of one's sex reasserting itself. A quick search for "top surgery"—the current euphemism for breast amputation—on the crowd-sourcing site GoFundMe shows over 37,000 results. As top surgeries cost between $5,000 and $10,000, the money generated from the people using GoFundMe alone (presumably only a fraction of overall surgeries) will be almost $300 million. Double mastectomies are currently being performed on girls as young as thirteen.[21]

One intervention pushed by activists, and increasingly embraced by medical professionals, is the off-label use of Lupron, a drug that can halt the natural process of puberty in children. Lupron is a hormone therapy approved for men with prostate cancer and women with endometriosis. Prescribing it to children has not been rigorously studied or FDA sanctioned. We are actively experimenting on our own children.

In 2017, the Endocrine Society, the leading international professional organization in the field of endocrinology, released new guidelines of care for adolescents with gender dysphoria. These revised standards of care state that the job of endocrinologists is now to "medically affirm"

---

[21] Johanna Olson-Kennedy et al., "Chest Reconstruction and Chest Dysphoria in Transmasculine Minors and Young Adults: Comparisons of Nonsurgical and Postsurgical Cohorts", *JAMA Pediatric* 172, no. 5 (2018): 431–36, https://doi.org/10.1001/jamapediatrics.2017.5440.

dysphoric minors by providing puberty suppression drugs and cross-sex hormones. Dr. Will Malone, an endocrinologist, was present at the national meeting when these guidelines were released. He was confused at the sudden redirection, particularly because these guidelines would result in the almost certain sterilization of the patient, in addition to other irreversible effects. When he first heard the guidelines, Dr. Malone assumed he must have missed some "landmark study", some "stunning piece of evidence" that could "shift the landscape" so radically in order to justify the directive that "mental health support and psychotherapy is out and affirmation is in."[22]

He was shocked to discover there is no such evidence. This monumental shift in clinical practice was supported by only a single, tiny, uncontrolled study with low-quality evidence from the Netherlands. According to Dr. Malone, "the quality of evidence is so low" that these protocols should be considered experimental therapies, not accessible to the public except through controlled trials. However, no such trials currently exist. Dr. Malone is emphatic: endocrinologists who follow these guidelines are "engaged in experimental medicine", and "the consequence of that is that people will be harmed. And that's what we're seeing."

The Danish study cited as evidence to support the affirmation model, also known as the Dutch protocol, was based on only fifty-five subjects.[23] These were all young people who had been struggling with gender dysphoria since childhood, and they were treated with puberty blockers and cross-sex hormones, followed by surgical removal of

[22] Sasha Ayad and Stella O'Malley, "Hormonal Interventions—From Fringe to Mainstream: A Conversation with Dr. Will Malone", *Gender: A Wider Lens Podcast*, January 8, 2021.

[23] Annelou L. C. de Vries et al., "Young Adult Psychological Outcome after Puberty Suppression and Gender Reassignment", *Pediatrics* 134, no. 4 (October 2014): 696–704, https://pediatrics.aappublications.org/content/134/4/696.

breasts, uterus, and ovaries for the girls, and removal of testes and vaginoplasty for the boys. The study had no control group—for example, a group treated with noninvasive methods—and did not assess physical health effects. Moreover, the results showed that gender dysphoria and negative body image actually *worsened* during puberty suppression. Most disturbingly, for one of the twenty-two adolescent boys, the vaginoplasty proved fatal. He died from necrotizing fasciitis after his surgery. Over a dozen other subjects could not continue due to health complications from the cross-sex hormones. In all, only forty of the original fifty-five completed the study. The final follow-up, which showed some alleviation of gender dysphoria and subjective happiness rates on par with peers, was only one year postoperation. There was no long-term assessment of the effectiveness of surgical reassignment.

Despite the low-quality evidence and a fatality rate of 4.5% for the boys, current medical practice not only follows, but actually *goes beyond* the recommendations of this uncontrolled study—urging earlier social transition, which is discouraged by the Dutch protocol, and applying the findings to youth with late-onset gender dysphoria, a newly emergent population that was not included in the original study. Thomas Steensma, one of the lead researchers behind the Dutch protocol, recently called into question whether the findings from his 2014 study should be used to treat the current cohort of young people. "We don't know whether studies we have done in the past can still be applied to this time", he said. "Many more children are registering, and also a different type."[24] Unfortunately,

---

[24] Berendien Tetelepta, "More Research Is Urgently Needed into Transgender Care for Young People: Where Does the Large Increase of Children Come From?", *AD* [Dutch newspaper], February 27, 2021, English translation at https://www.voorzij.nl/more-research-is-urgently-needed-into-transgender-care-for-young-people-where-does-the-large-increase-of-children-come-from/.

clinicians in the United States and elsewhere are not heeding these urgent calls for better research, because the force behind these seismic shifts in protocol is ideology, rather than evidence.

Activists and compliant clinicians peddle puberty suppression as a "pause button" that is fully reversible and without long-term effects. This unsubstantiated claim of complete reversibility used to be reflected on the British National Health Service's (NHS) website—until the wording was quietly changed, in May of 2020, to state:

> Little is known about the long-term side effects of hormone or puberty blockers in children with gender dysphoria. Although the Gender Identity Development Service (GIDS) advises this is a physically reversible treatment if stopped, it is not known what the psychological effects may be. It's also not known whether hormone blockers affect the development of the teenage brain or children's bones.[25]

This distancing from the GIDS recommendation happened against the backdrop of the Bell v. Tavistock case, which opened in October 2019 and concluded in December 2020. Keira Bell, a twenty-three-year-old woman, brought legal action against the NHS-GIDS for putting her on puberty blockers at the age of sixteen, initiating a path of medicalization that would include a double mastectomy and years of cross-sex hormones. Bell is now likely infertile because of the drug treatments, and her time on testosterone has given her male secondary sex characteristics that are irreversible, such as a deepened voice, Adam's apple, and facial hair.

---

[25] "Treatment: Gender Dysphoria", National Health Service, last updated May 28, 2020, https://www.nhs.uk/conditions/gender-dysphoria/treatment/; James Kirkup, "The NHS Has Quietly Changed Its Trans Guidance to Reflect Reality", *The Spectator*, June 4, 2020, https://www.spectator.co.uk/article/the -nhs-has-quietly-changed-its-trans-guidance-to-reflect-reality.

Bell won her case against the Tavistock Clinic in December 2020. The High Court found that children under sixteen are not able to legally consent to the use of puberty blockers. After carefully reviewing all available evidence, the Court declared that puberty-blocking drugs and cross-sex hormones are indeed experimental treatments with irreversible impacts, not yet backed by rigorous scientific study. In fact, the court's judgment revealed that GIDS had not even been accurately tracking the outcomes of their treatments; the results of their "experiment" were not even being assessed through careful controls. This landmark ruling makes plain the fact that these so-called treatments are based not on evidence, but on ideological assumptions about sex and gender and the privileging of *appearance* over physical health and functionality.[26]

Children who are given puberty blockers and then placed on cross-sex hormones *never go through puberty*. That natural process is completely halted. Not only does this lead to permanent sterility, it also arrests critical brain and bone development that occurs during puberty. The long-term ramifications of this artificial arrest are not yet known. It has been established, however, that the pediatric use of Lupron can lead to chronic pain from brittle bones

[26] In September 2021, the Court of Appeal overturned this initial judgment, appealing to prior legal precedent that "it was for doctors, not judges, to decide on the capacity of under-16s to consent to medical treatment." See "Quincy Bell and Mrs A v. The Tavistock and Portman NHS Foundation Trust: Judgment Summary", Judiciary of England and Wales, September 17, 2021, https://www.judiciary.uk/wp-content/uploads/2021/09/Bell-v-Tavistock-summary-170921.pdf. Bell plans to appeal this ruling to the Supreme Court. See Haroon Siddique, "Appeal Court Overturns UK Puberty Blockers Ruling for Under-16s", *Guardian*, September 17, 2021, https://www.theguardian.com /society/2021/sep/17/appeal-court-overturns-uk-puberty-blockers-ruling-for -under-16s-tavistock-keira-bell.

and joint deterioration, as well as teeth cracking and falling out.[27] Moreover, contrary to activist rhetoric, halting puberty does not just push pause, creating more time for discernment about transition. Nearly 100% of children put on puberty blockers proceed to take cross-sex hormones, with irreversible side effects.[28] Lupron is not a pause button, but a gateway.

The minors seeking these treatments are in great psychological distress, and, as a mother, I know that their parents must be desperate to alleviate that distress. The road to this hell of lifetime medicalization is, without a doubt, being paved with good intentions. That is no excuse for conducting a mass-scale, unassessed experiment on young people. The adults should know better, especially the medical professionals. I suspect, and hope, that the Bell v. Tavistock case is only the first ripple in a forthcoming tsunami of lawsuits.

Women and girls who pursue medical transition and then change course are left with irreversible effects that range from inconvenient to devastating—and those effects are not always disclosed beforehand. The first medical step is usually testosterone. According to the trans influencers on social media, "T" is something like a miracle drug; it can give one a sense of euphoria and energy and dissolve the layers of fat that tend to naturally settle around women's breasts and hips. Shifting the natural balance of female hormones away from estrogen leads to more masculinized features, like increased facial hair, male-pattern baldness,

---

[27] Christina Jewett, "Drug Used to Halt Puberty in Children May Cause Lasting Health Problems", *STAT News*, February 2, 2017, https://www.stat news.com/2017/02/02/lupron-puberty-children-health-problems/.

[28] Hannah Barnes and Deborah Cohen, "Tavistock Puberty Blocker Study Published after Nine Years", *BBC News*, December 11, 2020, https://www.bbc.com/news/uk-55282113.

a deepened voice. This all sounds pretty harmless, even appealing for someone wanting to appear male.

What's happening within the body is a different story. Starved of estrogen, the female reproductive organs begin to break down, becoming dry, hardened, fused, inflamed, and prone to infection.[29] This increasing atrophy in the uterus and vagina can be extremely painful, making something as simple as walking a difficult feat. After several years on testosterone, the atrophy typically worsens to the point that a hysterectomy is recommended. In short: testosterone slowly kills the female reproductive organs until they have to be surgically removed.

Testosterone, despite being a Schedule III controlled substance, is easy to obtain. The medical industry has adopted an "informed consent" model for dispensing these drugs, which means that someone can walk into a clinic, sign a consent form, and walk out with life-altering drugs. No diagnosis is necessary, and the "informed" part of the consent is not always thorough. In the United States, Planned Parenthood has become a prime distributor of what they call "femininizing and masculinizing medications".[30] Planned Parenthood prides itself on its "low-barrier, 'informed consent' model", which does not require a referral from a medical provider. Their website lists possible effects of testosterone, focusing on

---

[29] See M. Baldassarre et al., "Effects of Long-Term High Dose Testosterone Administration on Vaginal Epithelium Structure and Estrogen Receptor-α and -β Expression of Young Women", *International Journal of Impotence Research* 25 (2013): 172–77. See also Juno Obedin-Maliver, "Pelvic Pain and Persistent Menses in Transgender Men", UCSF Transgender Care, June 17, 2016, https://transcare.ucsf.edu/guidelines/pain-transmen.

[30] "Gender Affirming Hormone Care", Planned Parenthood Columbia Willamette, last accessed October 5, 2021, https://www.plannedparenthood.org/planned-parenthood-columbia-willamette/patient-resources/our-services/gender-affirming-care.

the external changes (muscle bulk, beard growth). The most unpleasant side effect listed is the possibility of acne and alopecia. Atrophy and sterilization are not mentioned at all.[31]

The affirmation model of care has essentially created a new product that is fueling increased market demand. In 2010, there were six gender clinics in the United States that dealt with referrals for treating gender dysphoria with cross-sex hormones, among other interventions. Now, there are sixty-five such clinics.[32] This is a 1,200% increase in a decade. These official gender clinics do not include the much higher numbers of community clinics, like Planned Parenthood, which dispense cross-sex hormones on an informed-consent basis.

Mackenzie, a young American detrans woman, went to Planned Parenthood for her testosterone. As promised, the process was low barrier. She knew her voice would deepen, but here is something Planned Parenthood didn't disclose: testosterone deepens the voice by causing vocal cords to lengthen and thicken. Mackenzie, a slim female, does not have a neck made to accommodate thick vocal cords, and now her voice tires easily; her throat hurts if she talks for long periods. Before her transition, she loved to sing. Now, singing is difficult, and her vocal range is stunted. During her transition process, Mackenzie experienced profound dissociation from her own body. Part of her journey back has involved reconnecting with her body through meditation, exercise, and making art. She thinks of her body as a friend now, rather than an object

---

[31] "Gender Affirming Hormone Care", Planned Parenthood of the Great Northwest and the Hawaiian Islands, last accessed October 5, 2021, https://www.plannedparenthood.org/planned-parenthood-great-northwest-hawaiian-islands/patient/services-transgender-patients.

[32] Ayad and O'Malley, "Hormonal Interventions".

to be constantly scrutinized. She is trying to learn how to sing again.[33]

Shortly after hearing Mackenzie's story, I came across other detransitioners who spoke of the same vocal injury. One woman posted an online video of herself singing "I Dreamed a Dream", urging the viewers to rethink transition if they wanted to maintain a singing voice. Nothing that can be gained from transition is worth that loss, she wrote.

As I listened to her sing, I felt swept away: first, by the beauty of her voice, deep and rich, wavering with gorgeous vibrato. Initially, I wasn't sure what she meant about her voice being ruined. Then her voice began to catch, cracking on the higher notes, wobbling like a pubescent boy's voice as she slid into the lower range. I watched her press a hand against her throat during some of the notes, as if stretching to reach them caused her pain.

Yet even in the midst of those glitches, the occasional botched notes, I became aware that I was witnessing a deeper kind of beauty, the beauty of a woman being herself, free from artifice: short hair swooped to the side, a trace of moustache on her lip, tattoos peeking over the collar of her T-shirt—no longer running from her imperfections, but learning to make music with them.

---

[33] "Mackenzie's Detransition Story", interview by Benjamin A. Boyce, April 4, 2020, in *Calmversations with Benjamin Boyce*, podcast, April 4, 2020, https://anchor.fm/boyceofreason/episodes/235--Mackenzies-Detransition-Story-eccosu.

Wholeness

I have given birth four times. Five, if you include the tiny body, no longer living, that was released from my womb at only ten weeks. The other four pregnancies bloomed to full term, my body stretched by a cumbersome metamorphosis, in which I am the cocoon. After the baby comes, once the chrysalis opens to unveil the face of a new human being, I feel shipwrecked, flung onto the shore in a state of limp exhaustion, not by the sea, but by my own terrible undulations. Thus begins the long season of postpartum *aftermath*, a grueling stretch of time that no one really talks about, that never appears on screen and is etched on few pages.

After each of my births, there is a moment when I am able to hobble to the toilet on my own, a massive pad pressed between my legs to catch the gush of blood that comes when I stand upright. I have to shuffle past a mirror to get there, and I can't help but look at the stranger I see, as if she is a monstrous Gorgon and I am trapped by her gaze. I see a body that doesn't look like me, that never matches how I appear in dreams or my own mental image. She has a dazed, half-crazed look, like she's just crawled out from the underworld; her breasts hang down, already beginning to harden with milk; her womb protrudes, emptied now but swollen nonetheless, as it will continue to be, for months. She fills me with disgust, that postpartum Medusa. She is grotesque and excessive, bleeding and leaking and saddled with flesh. I try to forget her, but she is there in every mirror, staring back at me when I expect to see myself.

With her comes a quiet terror that seeps slowly into my mind, like rising bathwater, until I'm submerged. Every sudden sound becomes a threat. Especially the crying—when the baby screams, I feel zaps of electricity in my brain, jolts of panic that sometimes get so bad I seek pain to release the tension, pricking the skin on my arm with a needle or stabbing my thigh with a key until it purples. Then my panic eases, giving way to a pervasive shame that irradiates my whole being like magma. There are moments of calm and even bliss, yes—but how quickly these can be shattered, how suddenly I can collapse into self-loathing and fear, how utterly this black flag can unfurl and block out the light.

In this state, my own mind becomes a predator. Thoughts invade my skull like a corkscrew, turning and turning until I can't pull them out. They strike in moments of quiet, like during Mass, and instead of Christ in the elevated Host I'm seeing a gunman burst in from the back of the church, and everyone's cowering under the pews, and I try to hide my baby, but he's strapped to me and crying and the gunman can hear him, and there's no way out; my flesh can't stop the bullet that will pierce us both.

This is what it's like for me, the aftermath of birth. Even now, as I write this, almost nine months postpartum, I still can't look at myself in the mirror without feeling disgust and a desire to punish my body, to starve it into submission. When I get out of the bath, I stand off to the side, hiding from my own reflection. I never thought, until recently, to compare my postpartum body dysmorphia to gender dysphoria. I am not plagued by the desire to be a man, that's true. Nonetheless, the more obviously female my body becomes, the more discomfort I feel.

Post-maternity, I long to embody a fantasy of womanhood divorced from femaleness, a woman who is hard-bodied, straight-hipped, and unbreasted, whose womb is imperceptible, unassertive. Even while I enjoy the skin-to-skin intimacy of breastfeeding, my breasts feel like interlopers, artificial appendages.

The acuteness of the dualism I feel, the disintegrated sense of self, is not unlike the descriptions I have heard from women who have identified as trans at one point or another. I do not pretend that my experience gives me full insight into the transgender experience—it does not—but when I hear women talk about gender dysphoria, I feel an echo in myself, an inner voice that whispers, *I know what that feels like.* Unlike the dysphoria of many of these women, however, mine is an acutely postpartum phenomenon and, at least thus far, tends to resolve when I stop breastfeeding and my body deflates like a balloon. Accepting the truth and goodness of my femaleness does not immediately resolve episodes of bodily dysphoria, but it does, at least most of the time, keep me from self-harm.

It took years and multiple births to accept that my invasive thoughts and self-loathing were pathological, a clear sign of postpartum anxiety and depression. My first instinct was to resist the label, to power through on my own strength, teeth clenched. I hunkered down in an alcove of denial, shielding myself from reality—the reality of my maternal body and the reality of my mental illness.

Self-Harm as Self-Care

According to Laura Reynolds, a former trans-identified woman, the gender paradigm has "rebranded self-harm as self-care".[1] This is yet another contortion of language with devastating consequences. As discussed in the previous chapter, clinical guidelines for gender dysphoria have shifted in recent years toward the affirmation model of care, which unquestioningly affirms a patient's interpretation of his or her condition. This seems to be the lone corner of psychology where the typical approach to psychological distress is upended, where practitioners are encouraged to take a patient's self-assessment at face value, rather than testing that assessment against reality.

What would it look like, I wonder, to take a so-called "affirmative" approach to my own mental illness? What would it sound like for a therapist to affirm my perception of reality? "Why yes, you should be hypervigilant at all times, especially during Mass, just in case a gunman shows up. You are in constant danger; your baby could die at any moment. Yes, your breasts aren't *really* part of you since you feel so disconnected from them. In fact, you might consider amputating them, so your reflection doesn't bother you anymore. And yes, if you feel like you are a terrible mother, I'm sure that you are."

You may think I'm being flippant here, because those responses seem so absurd, the dire opposite of therapeutic. Yet when I listen to the stories of detransitioners, this is often how they describe their experiences with affirmative care. The affirming doctors and therapists do not explore other causes or potential solutions but send the patient straight down the medical transition track.

One young woman, Grace, opted to inform her affirming doctor that she'd decided to detransition—a gutsy

[1] "Renegotiating Womanhood: A Detrans Story, with Laura", interview by Benjamin A. Boyce, January 21, 2020, YouTube video, 1:15, https://www.youtube.com/watch?v=4DOUcpFxKKw.

move that most detransitioners understandably don't make.[2] Grace explained to her doctor that she regretted her top surgery and years on cross-sex hormones, that these so-called treatments had brought her "pain, regret, and grief". The doctor acknowledged that Grace would have benefited from someone offering a solution other than transition—then bafflingly told her, "I don't see that as my role." What did the doctor see as her role? Total affirmation, and only affirmation: if a patient says she has gender dysphoria, give that as an official diagnosis and prescribe cross-sex hormones. Grace's doctor put the responsibility for diagnosis entirely on Grace—and also the blame when things went south. Grace had rushed into getting a mastectomy, the doctor said, a surgery for which the doctor had written an official recommendation.

Grace's experience with an affirming therapist was no better. When Grace said she was questioning her gender, the therapist recommended that Grace start binding her breasts, a practice that can lead to chest and back pain, difficulty breathing, and skin lesions. "That turned out to be the worst possible advice she could have given me", Grace said. Binding caused physical pain and made her dissociation from her body even worse. "After a few months of binding", she said, "I really wanted top surgery so I could stop binding."

When Grace went to a doctor for possible ADHD, the response was a "robust battery of tests" prior to diagnosis, and Grace was not put on medication until her eating disorder was in remission. With gender dysphoria, however, Grace was offered no robust assessment. She was not

[2] Carey Callahan (@mariacatt42), "Talking about Talking to Doctors", Medium, August 26, 2019, https://medium.com/@mariacatt42/talking-about-talking-to-doctors-49778915ed4.

evaluated for any comorbid conditions prior to being diagnosed and prescribed life-altering drugs and surgery. Grace
had a history of depression, isolation, sexual trauma, and
disordered eating, but none of this was explored by her
doctor or therapist in an effort to understand better the
source of her pain.

In story after story, I hear descriptions of complex mental distress that is attributed to a single source, gender,
and "treated" through the unproven, catch-all solution
of medical transition. I am not surprised that people latch
onto the notion of transition as a panacea for all their problems. The idea of a straightforward and decisive solution to
layers of psychological distress would be tantalizing to anyone. What's surprising to me are the clinicians, thought-
lessly trotting down the affirmation route like lemmings,
unconcerned by the lack of high-quality evidence justify-
ing medicalization. The affirmation model departs from
proven therapeutic approaches like cognitive behavioral
therapy, which tests a patient's perceptions against objective facts and evaluates cognitive distortions.

Gender dysphoria needs to be acknowledged and treated
as a psychological illness. I understand the resistance to language of disorder and pathology, motivated by a fear that
such language is stigmatizing. I understand, but I disagree.
To reclassify *disorder* as *order* forecloses the possibility of
recovery. I think of my own battles with anxiety, depression, self-harm. I don't want someone telling me those
things are normal and good. I want to be healed. I think
of Jesus in the Gospels, healing people from all kinds of
maladies. They cry out to him, reach for him, call upon
him, potently aware of their need for healing. We should
not resist the language of pathology here. What we must
resist is the stigma, the othering, of those who struggle
with mental illness. We should normalize the *experience* of

this struggle, but not the illness itself. And when I speak of those who struggle, I include myself among them.

Helena Kerschner, a woman who identified as trans for several years, has written pointedly about the "underground madhouse" of transgender healthcare, which is shaped by ideology rather than sound evidence.[3] Helena went to an informed consent clinic when she wanted to start cross-sex hormones. Even though she disclosed in the intake interview that she suffered from debilitating depression and had ideated about suicide as recently as three days prior, she was immediately given synthetic testosterone with no psychological evaluation—a powerful drug that can cause mood disruption.[4] She was not told about serious side effects, such as the vaginal atrophy she later developed. Helena now advocates for "compassionate and evidence-based care", care that attends to the whole person. "Truly compassionate, life-saving care", she writes, "would be to take an individualized approach with each patient and tend fully and as nonideologically as possible to the mental, emotional, and physical wellness of the entire human being."[5]

The affirmation model, while often motivated by good will, is ultimately unethical. It is dependent upon a diminished, dualistic model of personhood. The goodness, wholeness, and givenness of the body is discarded. The body is seen merely as an inert object, upon which an idealized sense of self is projected. This approach inverts the very definition of health, by pursuing a "treatment" that

[3] Helena Kerschner, "At What Cost? Trans Healthcare, Manipulated Data, and Self-Appointed Saviors", *New Discourses*, August 6, 2020, https://newdiscourses.com/2020/08/trans-healthcare-manipulated-data-self-appointed-saviors/.

[4] Helena Kerschner (@lacroicsz), Twitter, July 16, 2019, https://twitter.com/lacroicsz/status/1151238925698195456.

[5] Kerschner, "At What Cost?"

makes a healthy body ill, actively disrupting the delicate balance of the endocrine system in ways that have cascading and harmful effects. Invasive surgeries on healthy genitalia are often irreversible and involve short-term pain and long-term complications. The affirmation approach encourages violence to the healthy body rather than carefully working through the underlying causes of psychological distress and considering ways to manage that distress that do not cause physical harm. In this model, the body is the scapegoat, blamed as the sole source of one's pain and sacrificed on the altar of self-will.

What would it look like to approach a person in the depth of his complexity? In the fullness of her dignity? Such an approach would first seek to understand whether the person is actually suffering from gender dysphoria or whether there is something else going on. Classically, gender dysphoria manifests in early childhood and, in the vast majority of cases, resolves through the process of puberty.[6] In cases of late or sudden onset, it's unlikely that there is an underlying neurological condition. I've heard stories from women who experienced childhood dysphoria and never transitioned; I've heard stories from girls who transitioned without experiencing true dysphoria. Even if there are patterns and mutual echoes among these stories, none are exactly alike. Each person must be approached in her unique situation.

What would it look like to take concrete reality, especially the healthy body, seriously? To see the body as integral to the self? What would it look like to "test" a person's

---

[6] Multiple studies have demonstrated a high rate of desistance. See, for example, Thomas Steensma et al., "Factors Associated with Desistance and Persistence of Childhood Gender Dysphoria: A Quantitative Follow-up Study", *Journal of the American Academy of Child and Adolescent Psychiatry* 52, no. 6 (June 2013): 582–90. This study showed a desistance rate of 84%.

assumptions against that reality, to lead him into a grounded consideration of material existence, rather than pretending that matter does not matter? What if we embraced this as a guiding principle: *do not harm a healthy body*?

What would it look like to gently question a patient's assumptions about sex stereotypes rather than reinforce them? To encourage a healthy exploration of one's distinctive personhood—to give a girl freedom to live out her girl-ness, and a boy his boy-ness, in a unique and unrepeatable way? This, too, is part of God's creative vision. When sexed identity is grounded in the body, rather than confined to stereotypical mimicry, we are freer to be who we are.

By now I've made it clear that I disagree with trans-gender anthropology, namely its denial of the sacramental principle that *the body reveals the person*. Nonetheless, in every desire can be found a desire for something good, even if that good desire becomes distorted or aimed at the wrong thing. Trans identities signal a longing for *wholeness*, for an integrated sense of self, in which the body *does* reveal the person. This desire is fundamentally a good one; it reflects the truth of the human being as a unity of body and soul. The error comes in thinking that this integration has to be achieved through artifice, through violence against the body, rather than recognizing that we are integrated by our very nature. The lie—*I have to force my body to reveal my true self*—supplants the truth: *the body I am is always already revealing my personhood*.

This enduring desire for integration and wholeness can be harnessed, I think, as a bridge from a dualistic anthropology to a holistic one: a bridge from self-rejection to self-acceptance. In many transition stories, I hear a fundamental desire to escape the self. The allure of transition is about not self-expression but self-destruction, and the creation of a new persona altogether. I can see how intoxicating this must be, especially to adolescents. How I would have leapt at the chance to be someone other than myself in the throes of teendom. My intermittent suicidal ideation as a teenager was not so much about the desire to be dead, but the desire to stop being me, to self-immolate and rise again like a phoenix.

The affirmation model cannot offer true self-acceptance, unless the body is no longer considered part of the self. Choosing a lifetime of medicalization in order to maintain an illusion of cross-sex identity is not "being who you really are". The affirmation model is self-denial masquerading as self-acceptance. Because *our bodies are ourselves*, what is being "affirmed", ultimately, is the patient's self-hatred.

Some of the most vocal critics of medical transition I've encountered are gays and lesbians who are concerned that the transgender phenomenon is a socially lauded form of conversion therapy, an attempt to "correct" the problem of same-sex desire by altering a person's sex. Scott Newgent, the trans-identifying activist I mentioned in the chapter "Artifice", initially pursued gender transition in order to appease her girlfriend's devout Catholic family. In an essay for *Newsweek*, Newgent wrote, "It took me 48 years to realize I transitioned because I never wholeheartedly accepted being a lesbian."[7] While some people have more fluid sexual desires, there are certainly people for whom the directionality of attraction is fixed toward the same sex. Whether they choose to identify as gay or not, true self-acceptance must include that part of their personhood. To have communion with God—with anyone—we must bring our whole selves.

[7] Scott Newgent, "We Need Balance When It Comes to Treating Gender Dysphoric Kids. I Would Know", *Newsweek*, February 9, 2021, https://www.newsweek.com/we-need-balance-when-it-comes-gender-dysphoric-kids-i-would-know-opinion-1567277.

Some Christians might be concerned that I'm taking this line of argument, that by emphasizing the need to accept same-sex desire, I am rejecting the Church's teaching on sexual morality. That would be a misinterpretation. I believe that Christianity holds the truth about human sexuality, and I've structured my life around that truth. Right now, that looks like a long stretch of abstinence in order to avoid having another baby before my cycles are consistent enough to track again. I know that having another baby right now would threaten my mental health, and I need to be stable and present for my family. I'm ordering my sex life in deference to the intrinsic connection between sexual intercourse and human existence. I try to live in harmony with that connection, rather than in denial of it. This is not a path of pure repudiation, of negation—that would not be sustainable. My abstinence is an expression of love: for my husband, my children, and myself, as well as love for the divine ordering of creation.

One of the most beautiful elements of Christianity is its acceptance of desire as *good*, unlike Buddhism, say, which sees desire as fundamentally a source of suffering. There's a holy side to every longing. The trick is learning how to find it, learning how to channel our desires toward a good higher than sexual gratification. Erotic attraction for the same sex does not have to be, from a Catholic Christian perspective, a source of suffering and self-negation. Through the alchemy of grace, this can be a gift, like all of the beautiful contradictions that, taken together, make up every personality. Part of the work of conversion is learning to love who you are, because you've been made for love, and made *by* Love—a Love that dreamed you up and, in this and every moment, sings the song of your existence.

Truth-in-Love

Back in 2014, I remember talking with a friend from graduate school who, at the time, was completing a Ph.D. program on the East Coast. Josephine is French, queer, thoughtful, and one of the only people I've ever met whose eyes actually smile. I was worried that she would be reproachful about my then-recent Catholic conversion, but it didn't seem to bother her. She treated me, as always, with warmth and generosity. I remember listening to her description of the LGBT+ scene in New York City, how rapidly the transgender phenomenon was ramping up, especially among young people. "You don't see butch lesbians anymore", she said, "not under the age of 40." I remember feeling saddened by this, disturbed that there was a certain genre of womanhood that was quietly being erased.

While I was in the process of writing this book, Josephine contacted me out of the blue, and we met for a chat over Zoom. The first part of our conversation consisted of mutual confessions: Josephine, an atheist, was working on a book that kept pulling toward the idea of incarnation, which in her European academic milieu was a major faux pas. "Mentioning Catholicism in a remotely positive way is just *not done*", she said, laughing. I explained to her my own book project, which pushes back against the gender paradigm.

This was not much of a confession, at first. She acknowledged the dangers of gender nonconforming kids being "thrown into a framework" that leads them unnecessarily to the path of medicalization. "But some kids *are* transgender", she said. "That's just a reality." I could feel a chasm forming between us along with the immediate temptation to ignore it, to pretend it wasn't there. I was beginning to fear the moment when Josephine would realize we were not standing on the same side of the precipice. This moment came when I admitted that I was not convinced that medical transition was ever a good thing. "Even for adults?" she asked. I nodded, and then we were out of the safe zone. I could sense a slow dawning on her end of the realization that my views would fall into the category of what she considered to be transphobic.

This part of the conversation began with a discussion of *incarnation* and a shared recognition that this notion expresses the idea of body and spirit united, as "always together", to use Josephine's words. "Doesn't a transgender anthropology conflict with that idea?" I ventured. "How can the body and spirit be one, if that union must be inflicted on the body?" "Inflicted"—that was the word I used, and she reacted strongly to it.

"How is a sex change more of a punishment on the body than the punishment of having to try and have sex with a body that isn't right?" she asked. "Wouldn't that be even more traumatizing?" For some people, she argued, transition is the path to self-acceptance. "Sex change can be a gift to one's own incarnation", she said.

I wish I'd had the clarity and nerve to respond in that moment, to say that sexual gratification is not an end in itself, that incarnation is not something we create but something we receive. In the moment, I wasn't sure what to say. I told her as much, and our conversation stalled into awkward silence. Josephine was voicing a side of this complicated story that I wanted to ignore: the fact that plenty of transgender people appear to be satisfied with their transitions. The evidence for this is often anecdotal, yes, due to the dearth of long-term studies on surgical reassignment outcomes. (The one long-term study that exists, in fact, shows a twenty-fold increase in suicidality *after* transition.)[8] There are well-adjusted transgender people in the world who find some relief through transition. That is true, and Josephine was right to point this out.

After the lull, I decided to tease out Josephine's perspective. "How do you define 'woman'?" I asked her.

"Woman!" she said. "Ah, woman is *magic*." We laughed together at this; her effusiveness warmed me, pulling me out of the shell I'd ducked into. She went on, "There's something problematic in deciding from the outset what 'woman' is. Every category is a simplification of multiplicity. Each person who is a woman relates to it differently."

"So, do you see 'woman' as a kind of archetype, or ...?"

She thought for a moment. "No, not an archetype—woman is an *art form*."

I smiled at this idea. "OK, so how does the art form of 'woman' differ from the art form of 'man'?"

"Man is not an art form!" She laughed at this, and I had to laugh too, even though I disagreed, thinking passingly of Michelangelo's *David*—more so the resplendent bodies of my sons, my husband. Man is a magnificent art form.

"I think about 'woman' like I think about 'lesbian'", Josephine continued with a more serious tone. She described the standard nominalist position that many feminists hold—the idea that categories like "woman" and

---

[8] C. Dhejne et al., "Long-Term Follow-Up of Transsexual Persons Undergoing Sex Reassignment Surgery: Cohort Study in Sweden", *PLOS ONE* 6, no. 2 (2011): article no. e16885. This study concludes: "Persons with transsexualism, after sex reassignment, have considerably higher risks for mortality, suicidal behaviour, and psychiatric morbidity than the general population. Our findings suggest that sex reassignment, although alleviating gender dysphoria, may not suffice as treatment for transsexualism, and should inspire improved psychiatric and somatic care after sex reassignment for this patient group."

"lesbian" are constructs, but necessary for activism. "You need the category for political struggle", she said, "keeping in mind that it's a fiction."

"I guess that's where I disagree", I said. "I don't think 'woman' is a fiction; I think we need a definition of 'woman' that is grounded in the body. If it's grounded in the bodily potentiality of femaleness, being a woman doesn't have to be about conforming to sex stereotypes. There's something freeing about that."

Josephine hesitated. "Yes, I do want to think that 'woman' is grounded in the body in some way", she admitted. "I'm not entirely satisfied with my own answers!"

I realized then that we were feeling the same tension, but from different angles. I was unwilling to compromise my convictions that the sexed body matters and is integral to the self. But I felt the draw of taking an affirming political stance, in order to make intelligible another conviction: that trans-identifying people are beloved and made in the image of God. Josephine, in contrast, was unwilling to betray her political convictions, even though she felt a pull toward an embodied understanding of woman. We found ourselves at an impasse.

As a Catholic Christian, I am beholden to a twofold truth: the dignity of every human being and the dignity of the sexed human body. These truths are entwined, inseparable. A transgender anthropology says, whether implicitly or explicitly, that I can only affirm the former by rejecting the latter. I can only proclaim a trans person's dignity by agreeing that his or her body is a lie. This puts me in a double bind, a no-win scenario. If I say that sex matters, I'm put on a one-way train to presumptive transphobia. If I say that sex doesn't matter, I'm betraying the truth of my own embodiment and the truth of God's self-revelation. I need to make peace with being misunderstood, because both prongs of the twofold truth need to be spoken—with compassion, to be sure, but spoken nonetheless.

Debates about gender and sexuality, especially in Christian circles, tend to split into two opposing camps, one staking a flag on Love, the other on Truth. I feel this apparent tension most painfully around the use of language. To affirm the dignity and personhood of a trans-identifying person, one is expected to use pronouns that align with the chosen gender, rather the given sex. To "misgender" someone is seen as an act of violence, an erasure of existence. I understand this argument. A transgender identity is not primarily rooted in material reality, but in language. This is why there is so much fervor over words, a concerted effort to use language in a way that reflects transgender anthropology. If I use the word "he" to refer to a male who identifies as a transwoman, I am denying his existence *as a woman*. Of course, I am also simultaneously *affirming* his existence as a man, and as a human being.

Using sex-based pronouns, rather than gender-based pronouns, is undoubtedly disruptive and likely offensive to most trans-identified people. Such a move could close the door to a relationship with that person from the outset. Yet, if I use pronouns that conflict with sex, I am assenting to an untruth. More than assenting, in fact; through my own words I am actively *participating* in a lie.

Speak the truth in love. This is a phrase I hear bandied about, a phrase I find myself turning to, whenever I feel pulled in these opposing directions, these at-odds affirmations. This phrase too easily becomes a platitude, simple and trite, a scriptural fragment conveniently used to carve a party line. These words come from Paul's Letter to the Ephesians, chapter four—a passage, it turns out, that is about not partisanship and division, but wholeness.

The chapter begins with a litany of unity: one body, one Spirit, one hope, one Lord, one faith, one baptism, one God, who is "above all and through all and in all." This is a passage about ecclesiology, the nature of the Church, how the Christian community draws together all kinds of individuals, each with different gifts, into a cohesive whole. This whole is called *a body*—that's the metaphor Paul uses here, relying on the integral reality of the body to illustrate his vision of the Church. The personal wholeness of body and soul is not simply a foundational tenet of Christian anthropology; it also grounds Christian ecclesiology. "Speaking the truth in love," Paul writes, "we are to grow up in every way into him who is the head, into Christ, from whom the whole body, joined and knit together by every joint with which it is supplied, when each part is working properly, makes bodily growth and upbuilds itself in love."[9] Truth and love are one, because they spring from the same source, the fountainhead of Christ, the Incarnate Word.

God's truth is love, and God's love is truth. If we ever find ourselves in a situation where we are sacrificing one for the other, we've wandered off the narrow track. In his First Letter to the Corinthians, Paul gives us an image of what pseudo-truth *sans* love sounds like: a clanging cymbal, a cacophonous mess. Perhaps the counterimage—faux love *sans* truth—would be an advertising jingle, simpering and circular. Love divorced from truth descends into mere flattery. It is not loving to validate a lie. It is not loving to participate in someone's self-deception. To learn how best to love someone, we must be willing to reckon with the truth of the human person, which is found not merely in our self-written stories, but in the overarching story of the whole.

[9] Ephesians 4:15–16.

When it comes to men and women, we need to use *reality-based language*. Within the gender paradigm, words are wielded to enforce a framework that distorts the reality and goodness of the body, particularly its sexed duality. This distortion perpetuates itself by hijacking language. I feel the temptation to acquiesce, to say the affirming thing, the unoffensive thing. I am also aware that, in doing so, I secure myself as part of the in crowd, the non-bigots, the illuminati on history's right side. Less selfishly, I also want to express my belief that a trans person has infinite worth and is made for loving communion, like all human beings. Because of this, my affections and sentiments pull strongly in the direction of affirmation.

Whenever possible, I avoid pronouns when directly speaking with or writing about trans-identifying people, in order to avoid unnecessarily alienating someone I am called to love. But I can't go further than this. Each time I think about making a full linguistic concession, something stops me. I run into a hard boundary, a line my conscience has marked not in sand, but stone. To call a male "she" is a lie, an inversion of the reality that that word names, a reality I happen to belong to, one that I have not chosen, but that has chosen me. I object to the very concept of preferred pronouns, because pronouns do not name a preference. "She" names what I am, my female birthright, with all its blessings and burdens. To give away that word would be a kind of betrayal: of myself, my sex, and those bodily threads knit by nature and grace that bind us to Christ, and also to the earth, to all her teeming life.

Love-in-Truth

We are loved with an infinite love that bestows upon us an infinite dignity. The boundless love of God ennobles

every human person. Through the ever-present miracle of
the Incarnation, each of us has been taken up into the very
life of God. These words are my riff on the pontiff; I'm
playing with phrases that vibrate with beauty from Pope
Francis' letter *Evangelii gaudium*. In this letter, Pope Francis
describes what he calls *the art of accompaniment*, an art that
begins by teaching us "to remove our sandals before the
sacred ground of the other."[10]

Recently a mutual friend put me in touch with Adelynn, a vibrant young person who identifies as a transwoman. Addy, a devout Christian, was eager to speak with
me after listening to a podcast interview I'd done about
gender theory and Christian theology. And I was just as
eager to speak with Addy. In the course of writing this
book, I have spoken with a number of trans people who
hold a range of political and religious beliefs, but none of
them have a theologically traditional Christian perspective.
Either they aren't Christian at all, or they have drifted into
heterodoxy and perhaps out of the faith altogether. Addy,
then, is something of a unicorn—a young person who
embraces both orthodox Christianity and a trans identity.

I tell this to Addy as we launch into our first conversation over Zoom. "I've been trying to find someone, some
thinker, who can harmonize a Christian anthropology
with a trans anthropology, but—"

"There's no one", Addy cuts in, anticipating my next
words. "No one!"

Addy is working on this, though, drawing together
three theological threads in an attempt to make a positive
case for transition from a Christian perspective. The first
thread is a reading of the Fall that situates trans people
as living paradoxes, people who experience a disconnect

---

[10] Francis, encyclical letter *Evangelii gaudium* (The Joy of the Gospel)
(November 24, 2013), no. 169.

between mind and body that is a consequence of living in a world that has lost its original harmony. Addy returns to this theme repeatedly during our conversation, gesturing toward the promise of the resurrection, the restoration of all creation: "God will fix whatever he needs to fix, whether that's my head or my body." In this reading of the Fall, that reconciliation of body and mind might not be attainable in this life; the psychosomatic unity that should be present in each person is simply not there for some, and so the question becomes how to live, to survive, amidst that discordance.

This is where the second guiding thread comes in: What would promote preservation of the whole? In Addy's experience thus far, this preservation has come in the form of transition—specifically, almost six years of taking cross-sex hormones, after adopting a female social and legal identity in college. This is an example of what you might call a classic case of gender dysphoria, rather than the wave of rapid-onset gender dysphoria that is sweeping through teenagers today. Addy first experienced a sense of incongruence as a child, and that feeling persisted into young adulthood, when it manifested in debilitating physical symptoms, such as daily vomiting and severe underweight. Those symptoms have dissipated; Addy is now much more functional and, because of this, does not regret transition.

Still, the unresolved theological tensions are at times a source of unrest in Addy, who, unlike my younger self, is not hand-waving away the difficult questions in order to construct an easy, tailor-made theology that only affirms and never confronts. This is someone who is actively grappling with truth—like Jacob in the dead of night, wrestling with that mysterious divine being until daybreak, refusing to let go until he is blessed.

When Addy began transition, this refusal took the form
of a resolute vow: "I am not cutting myself off from the
church." The few hours spent in church on Sunday were
blissful, "a slice of heaven", like being momentarily trans-
ported out of the world and all its painful paradoxes. "I
didn't want to leave after the benediction", Addy tells me,
and this consolation kindled a desire to be in church more
regularly. "But it turns out that if you want to go to church
every day, the only real option is a Catholic Mass." So
that's where Addy went: Catholic Mass on the weekdays
and a vibrant multiethnic reformed church on Sundays.

This ardent commitment to the church has not always
been reciprocated. For most of our conversation, Addy is
upbeat and smiling, speaking words that reveal a deep love
for Christ and his people. But there are also flashes of pain,
glimpses into unhealed wounds—wounds of abandon-
ment and rejection. In relation to roots, Addy is an exile;
transitioning in college resulted in public shunning by the
church community, with no warning or attempt at reconciliation. That rejection was soon mirrored by Addy's own
family, and the resulting rupture has lasted for six years so
far. This brings us to the third thread, the recurrent presence of the outcast in Scripture and Christian history: the
eunuch, the leper—the person who doesn't fit in and is,
too often, exiled.

This aspect of Addy's experience exemplifies one approach Christians can take in response to those within the
gender paradigm—this is the way of ostracism, separation, a holy "us" opposed to an ousted "them". But this, I
would argue, is an approach that prizes truth to the exclu-
sion of love, and is thus a counterfeit truth. Even churches
that do not explicitly reject or shun people like Addy
have little to offer in terms of a positive vision of how to
live out the more challenging teachings of the Christian

life. As Addy puts it, the Church, for the most part, "is not coming alongside and saying, *this is how we will help you bear this.*"

I see in this story another possible model for Christians to follow as we navigate a confused and polarizing culture. After finishing college, Addy eventually ended up with a Catholic roommate. After experiencing so much rejection from Christians, Addy wasn't sure how this roommate would respond. But the roommate did something rather remarkable. Instead of being wary and suspicious, she was warm and friendly. Instead of telling Addy what to think and believe, she *asked* about Addy's perspective and how one can reconcile Christian theology with the choice to pursue transition. These questions, and the spirit in which they were asked, sparked rich and lengthy theological conversations between the roommates. Avoiding the easy extremes of condemnation on the one hand and fawning affirmation on the other, Addy's roommate chose to cultivate a relationship, to ask genuine questions, and eventually, to extend an invitation to Eucharistic Adoration.

Addy's face lights up at this part of the story, this initial encounter with adoration: "I *love* it!" Once again I'm struck by the beauty of Addy's heart—a heart like that of the bride in the Song of Songs, who calls out to her beloved, *draw me after you.*[11] This is what Christ is doing: patiently, lovingly, he is drawing Addy to himself.

The Christians in Addy's hometown show one possible response to those who identify as LGBT+. But Addy's roommate shows us a different, more Christlike way—the way of accompaniment rather than rejection; the way of love, rather than the way of fear.

[11] Song of Songs 1:4, New American Bible.

Accompaniment is a way of journeying with someone deeper into the heart of Christ. Contrary to the cliché, conversion is not a one-time zap; the Holy Spirit is not a fairy godmother who makes you insta-ready for the ball. Conversion is a steady pilgrimage, a long trek into the heart of God. There are detours and switchbacks along the way; none of us hike straight; none of us can manage alone. Accompaniment evokes this sense of conversion over time, as well as the need for community along the way. Pope Francis makes a distinction between accompaniment as a pilgrimage with someone versus a "sort of therapy supporting their self-absorption."[12] In other words, true accompaniment has a *telos*, a destination; it is ordered toward the highest love. While it should begin with affirmation of an individual's worth, it cannot end there. We must journey toward the source of that worth, wherein lies our peace.

When I made a sudden hairpin turn toward Catholicism at the age of thirty, I was *not* on board with many of the Church's teachings. I was not a typical, respectable Protestant, repelled by the macabre excess of Catholicism, her weeping statues and saints' bones, her gruesome crucifixes. I wanted a cross with a body hanging on it; I longed to open my lips and taste the Blood of Christ; I would have loved to touch Saint Catherine of Siena's desiccated head with my bare, trembling hands. But I didn't understand or welcome the Church's resistance to contraception, female priests, and same-sex marriage, and I became Catholic before having those questions resolved. My initial conversion was like going blind down a twisting slide and coming out head-first and breathless, eyes opened to a spinning, upside-down

---

[12] Francis, *Evangelii gaudium*, no. 170.

world. I didn't immediately adopt every Catholic teaching in my personal life. I skipped over the phrase *for us men* in the Creed. I was mostly trekking alone, with no Catholic family members or close friends to guide me. I was "accompanied" only by a former-student-turned-seminarian, Stephen, to whom I brought all my objections, my unresolved questions. I grilled him on contraception, the priesthood, sexuality. Most of the time his answers pissed me off, and I neither accepted nor dismissed them. I let them kick around in my head like pinballs, until, over a period of months, each of them pinged home.

If Stephen had come out pistols blazing, grilling me on my sex life, calling me out for skipping words in the Creed, dissuading me from attending Mass until my sin-duckies were all in a row—I might not have entered the Church at all. Or I might have stayed an ambivalent Catholic, defensive and suspicious, holding myself off from full communion with the truth. He didn't. He was open and patient; he listened to me; he took my concerns seriously, and he waited for me to come to him with my questions, rather than cornering me and forcing a conversation. When I did come to him, he was honest in his responses. He did not sugarcoat or equivocate; he spoke the difficult truths, in a spirit of nonjudgment. For this, I will always be grateful.

Even as we speak honestly about the machinations of the gender paradigm, we have to realize that there are real people, real lives, being churned up in its gears. We have to welcome these people into our parishes, into our families, into our communities. It is possible to judge whether an ideology is true or false—but we cannot judge persons; we have not been granted access to the inner chambers of the human heart. Each person's status before God is a mystery that cannot be known from without. We must critique the framework, in the appropriate time and place, while embracing those who are caught up in that framework, no matter how they look or sound.

We need to accept that men and women might not look like we expect them to look. If you happen to see someone who might be transgender, you still have no idea whether that person is in the midst of transition or detransition. Because some aspects of medical transition are irreversible, even a woman who has embraced her sex might still look transgender. She might always have masculinized features. That doesn't make her any less of a woman. Surgical reversals, even if desired, might not always be possible or could pose serious health risks.

Lee, a woman who suffered horrific sexual abuse as a child, medically transitioned late in life. She now regrets transition but has decided not to undergo reversal surgeries. "My body can't take it. I'm not sure I'd survive all the surgeries", she says. "I have to accept my body the way it is now. On the outside people see a little bloke. Inside I'm a traumatized little girl. But I'm more accepting of myself for the first time ever. I just wish I'd been helped to accept myself earlier." For people like Lee, self-acceptance means embracing the body as it currently is.[13]

Of course, the gender-atypical woman you see in your local parish might not be trans-identified at all. She might just be a woman who has short hair and likes to wear men's shirts. Both narrow-minded traditionalists and postmodern genderists fall prey to the same error: defining manhood and womanhood by stereotypical caricatures and policing those stereotypes, assessing how well individuals conform, or fail to conform, to a fantasized ideal. Part of countering

[13] Laura Dodsworth (@barereality), "The Detransitioners", Medium, August 18, 2020, https://medium.com/@barereality/the-detransitioners-72a4e01a10f9.

the gender paradigm must be a greater openness to the variability *within* the categories of man and woman. Think of Saint Joan the warrior, Saint Dominic the beggar—the gentleness of Saint Francis de Sales, the fortitude of Saint Catherine of Siena. One quick tour through the halls of the communion of saints reveals motley manifestations of feminine or masculine genius that defy a singular mold.

I was given ample room to meander in my journey toward the truth, and the winding path I took unfolded largely *within* the community of the Church, rather than outside a high, locked gate. The Church is not for ready-made saints. The Church is for sinners, doubters, half-brewed Christians, conversions-in-process, tipsy wagon-riders who tumble off and climb back on again. Our parishes must be places where the truth is preached, yes—and also places where people are allowed to fumble their way toward it, gradually being made new.

Gift

Daisy Chadra was a serious child—creative and intense, more temperamentally suited to windswept English moorland than midwestern American suburbia. But none of us choose the time or place we tumble into the world and enter the current of human history, and Daisy is no exception. Had she been born a century earlier, she might have become another Charlotte Brontë or George Eliot, women who penned their novels under male personas, wanting to be taken seriously as writers and thinkers. As a child, Daisy was a writer, too, churning out character-driven stories that always seemed to arrange themselves around male heroes. She tried to conjure convincing heroines, but they never took shape, and so she gave up trying.

From an early age, Daisy professed openly her desire to be a boy, and no matter how often her parents reassured her that she could live out womanhood in her own unique way, she remained unconvinced. When Daisy projected herself out toward the imagined horizon of the future, she didn't see an androgynous woman or a masculine woman—she didn't see a woman at all. She could only imagine herself growing into manhood.

"I had this vision of myself that seems pretty misogynistic when I think about it", she told me, "being this intellectual, stoic kind of person. I had this archetypal idea of myself that seemed inherently male."

Daisy does have a somewhat serious vibe; she speaks with deliberation, reaching for the best words to express a complex thought. There is also a warmth and brightness about her, an energy that quickens in her voice over the course of our conversation. If I had to choose a word to describe her, it wouldn't be *stoic* so much as *earnest*. She speaks about herself and her life from a place of grounded sincerity.[1]

I told Daisy when we spoke that she reminded me of Simone Weil—the early twentieth-century mystic who loved the Christian faith with as much intensity as she held herself away from its institutional body—a devout but self-exiled daughter of the Church. Weil was a heady intellectual, yes, and also a mystic with an open heart, waiting to be invaded by God. Weil was shaped by her time and also out of step with it. Whatever she did, she did with intensity. Daisy didn't come of age in the tumult between world wars like Weil or in the corseted Victorian era like Brontë and Eliot. She was born at the turn of the new millennium, hitting teendom alongside the ascendancy of Tumblr and YouTube. Her experience of herself and her identity was mediated not by strict moralism or Marxist revolution, but by the new wave of pop gender theory, a choose-your-own-adventure self. This framework, which has captured our cultural imagination, fragments personhood into mix-and-match categories of gender identity, gender expression, sexual orientation, and biological sex (to name a few). Instead of moving from girlhood into womanhood, she took a sharp detour at the

---

[1] My telling of Daisy's story is drawn from my personal interview with her, as well as her interview with Benjamin Boyce and a video on her own YouTube channel. Used with permission. See "DeTrans Stories: The Authenticity Quest with Daisy Chadra", interview by Benjamin A. Boyce, December 6, 2020, YouTube video, 1:10, https://www.youtube.com/watch?v=4EtS0146uQk. Daisy's video can be found here: "I'm Detransitioning", October 26, 2020, YouTube video, 26:55, https://www.youtube.com/watch?v=R_KD46_Ophg.

age of seventeen, the end of her junior year in high school, announcing to family and friends that she was not Daisy, but Ollie—not a woman, but a man.

This was 2015, when rates of adolescent transition first began to skyrocket. Like most teenagers, Daisy had immersed herself in the online world, using it as a therapeutic escape from real life and the turbulence of adolescence. This is where she first encountered trans influencers on social media, seeing in their stories something of herself. "I wanted their narrative to be my narrative", she said. "They had found their true selves, they were happy, they were attractive, they were successful in life, and those were things that I really wanted." She began to wonder if the missing piece to her own success and well-being could be attributed to a singular, fundamental cause: her gender. "The idea that I had just been living life as the wrong gender", she said, "and if I just correct that, I would be able to thrive, was really attractive to me."

Daisy began to adopt the language and framing of pop gender theory, translating her experience through the prism of its categories. Even though she was an atheist, she embraced the standard spiritual vernacular of transgender anthropology. "I have a male soul and a female body", she said, describing how she thought at that time. "They are contradicting each other, and I can't change my soul, so I have to change my body."

At first, Daisy was unsure about medical transition. Her dysphoria had never been acutely physical; she did not loathe her female body, but rather wanted to be perceived as a man, to be able to seamlessly adopt a male role in society. But coming out publicly as a trans man turned out to be the first step toward medicalization. She wanted to be taken seriously, and so she plunged into the process of medical transition. "I went into it full speed ahead", she

said, "maintaining the promise of some vague happiness in
my future."

As soon as she was eighteen, Daisy went to an informed-
consent clinic to begin cross-sex hormones. She thought
there would be some kind of psychological evaluation, but
there was no gatekeeping; within an hour or two of showing up at the clinic for the first time, she was given her
first shot of testosterone. Two years later, again with no
psychological evaluation, Daisy underwent a double mastectomy. She had just turned twenty.

Thus far, Daisy had few doubts about her transition.
"I was really jazzed when I started testosterone", she
laughed. Every perceivable change—a deepened voice,
budding facial hair—put her one step closer to complete
self-transformation. Her transition had a teleological bent,
driven toward a final goal, and each change along the way
was a foretaste of that final fulfillment. Listening to Daisy
describe her experience, I can understand how exhilarating
that must have felt, to perceive tangible metamorphosis in
real time, to watch a new form emerge from the material
of one's own body, to be both sculptor and statue at once.

The doubts came when she had finished the final step:
a legal name change. She was on cross-sex hormones,
which were masculinizing her body; she had adopted a
legal and social identity as a man; she had completed the
only surgeries she wanted to pursue. The process she had
embarked on was now complete. "I was waiting for that
final sigh of relief", she said.

It didn't come. In its absence—the absence of the fulfillment she had anticipated—doubts began to crowd in.
The vision of the future that had propelled her forward
was now her present, and she found herself, as she put it,
"staring into an abyss that should be a future". She was
devastated, carrying around a sick, sinking feeling in her

torso, haunted by the thought that she would never be complete. She was now faced with two options that each seemed unlivable: she had to either live with her transition or try to reverse it.

Initially, she chose the first option, keeping her doubts locked deep, confiding in no one. During this time, she struggled with severe body-image issues, acutely aware that her altered body still did not look like a man's. She now felt an inverse incongruence with her sex. Before transitioning, there was incongruence between her perceived "male soul" and female body. Now, she felt a schism between her female body and the whole male persona she had created. Unlike the initial dysphoria, this new incongruence was sharply physical and much more debilitating.

Transition is often framed as a do-or-die scenario. People wracked with dysphoria are told that if they do not transition, they will likely kill themselves, and if they regret their transition, they will likely kill themselves. This narrative can twist into a self-fulfilling prophecy. "If it had not been for this narrative", Daisy acknowledged, "I would have been able to get through the dysphoria and develop as my own person, learn to be myself in a more real and meaningful way." In the hell of self-doubt, the track of this grim prophecy kept playing in her head, and she became suicidal.

I want to pause here and emphasize something. Daisy is careful to stress that her experience is particular and not representative of all trans-identified people or even all detransitioners. I want to stress this, too. I am describing her story not to create a "just-so tale", but to highlight how our guiding frameworks give shape to our experiences and influence the ways we respond to them. This is something postmodernism gets right. The language we use, the explanatory narratives in which we are embedded—these shape how we interpret the world and how we choose to act within it.

Postmodernism's *hamartia* is assuming that there are *only* narratives, *only* lenses of interpretation, that no narrative can be truer than another, because there is no underlying ground of meaning. If there is such a ground, this means that we must evaluate our explanatory stories according to their correspondence with truth. Our lenses can illuminate, and they can also distort. Our narratives can reveal *that-which-is*, and they can occlude. Our language shapes our sense of reality, yes—and reality pushes back.

There is another thread of Daisy's story to pick up here, another transformation that was unfolding simultaneously: an interior, rather than exterior, metamorphosis.

Midway through her transition, around the age of twenty, Daisy began thinking about God. This was not a new thought, but one long dormant, an interest from her childhood that had quieted down during a teenage period of atheistic skepticism. She was in college now, majoring in communications, while taking courses in religion and philosophy. At first this God-thought was a purely intellectual pursuit; she was willing to believe in God's existence, but this was not necessarily a personal deity who cares and guides with intention.

Then the God-thought became a Christ-thought. She found herself fascinated with the person of Christ. "There's a sense of completion and wholeness to the narrative of Christ", she explained. Daisy started visiting churches, not as a believer but as a seeker. She passed as Ollie, cautiously hiding her trans identity, unsure whether she would be accepted or rejected by the Christians around her.

Daisy's growing interest in Christianity dovetailed with her escalating doubts about transition. She skirted around the edges of faith, remaining noncommittal. Listening to

Daisy tell her story, I find myself imagining two diagonal roads that begin at a far distance from one another and then run over the land until they converge at a shared point. This convergence of quests—the spiritual quest and the identity quest—happened in the spring of 2020, during the first wave of COVID lockdowns.

After trying for several months to recommit to transition, Daisy had begun opening up about her doubts, but only to virtual strangers she met on dates, still too afraid to admit her distress to anyone in her life. Now that she'd passed the last hurdle of transition, she had to reckon with the consequences of long-term testosterone. She'd already been taking it for three years, and she became increasingly aware that around the five-year mark, her reproductive organs would likely atrophy to the point of needing a hysterectomy. The door to biological motherhood was closing. Daisy's growing desire to one day have a child eventually outpaced the terror of detransition. "By that time", she told me, "doubts about transition were tormenting me day and night. And so I stopped taking T. I thought, I guess this is happening. I'm detransitioning."

Around the same time, Daisy decided to experiment with practicing Christianity, rather than eyeing it from a safe distance. She asked herself, "What do I want to get out of my study of Christianity? What is the goal here?" Desperate for some ground of meaning, she began to read Scripture and prayed: "God, show yourself to me." And he did. "For the first time, I knew what I believed, and I knew who I really was. I was God's", she said. "I belong to God."

It might be tempting to read this convergence of conversion and detransition in a simplistic, moralized way: trans person reads Bible, gets saved, feels guilty, stops being trans. That is "not even close to what happened", Daisy said. "How I felt about being trans wasn't *guilt*, like 'I'm sinning, I'm being bad, I'm being a sinful horrible person.' It was like: this is not right for you. This is not what you should be doing." The Christian frame that Daisy slowly entered into was not a punitive, legalistic one, a frame of cold tablets etched with condemnation—*you are nothing, your desires don't matter, you are innately depraved.* Instead, it was the recognition of a deeper desire. "Maybe there is an innate part of everyone that actually wants to live with God", she said. "And maybe I found that part of myself and have to nurture that part of myself." Her unwillingness to accept herself had become a "blockade" between herself and God, and when she decided to detransition, "some kind of veil was lifted, and I felt like I could go full throttle into my faith." This was not a negation of self, but a rediscovery; not a repudiation of identity, but an unveiling.

Wholeness

What I see happening in the convergence of Daisy's metamorphoses is not about rule-breaking and reproof, but rather entering into *a different way of seeing.* The first and most significant shift happens when Daisy began to see herself as a creation of God. Considering oneself as a being who is *created* moves the discussion of identity to new ground, setting the frame of a transcendent order—an order beyond the natural that sustains its existence and safeguards its meaning. To be a creature, rather than an accident, establishes the human person as a being-in-relation with the divine. We are not alone in the cosmos; always, whether we acknowledge it or not, whether we are aware or not, we live and move and have our being in God.

When we see the world as a created cosmos of which we are a part, this transfigures everything: embodiment, sex, suffering, freedom, desire—this is gathered up into an all-embracing mystery, an ongoing interplay between the human and divine. This imbues *all-that-is* with renewed significance. In the light of her createdness, Daisy's understanding of her sex changed from something arbitrarily assigned to "something that had purpose behind it". She no longer saw herself as her own creator, responsible for the work of self-fabrication. Once understood as *created*, selfhood, including one's sex, becomes a gift that can be accepted, rather than something that must be constructed. This initiates a different orientation to all of reality, even one's own body: a shift from *control* to *receptivity*.

We are coming full circle now, back to the beginning, to our earlier discussion of Genesis and the intrinsic connection between identity and purpose. Christianity—indeed, all ancient thought—is thoroughly *teleological*. The "whatness" of a thing, its essential identity, is connected to its purpose. In Aristotelian terms, this is known as the fourth or final cause, the final end toward which something is directed. The final cause is easy to discern with simple objects. The *telos* of a chair is to uphold a person in a seated position. A chair is designed to fulfill this singular purpose. What about human beings? What are we designed for?

The answer in the Babylonian Enuma Elish is servitude, to be slaves of the gods. The *telos* of humankind in this myth mirrors its portrayal of divinity: Marduk is a violent warrior, a conqueror; his creative power is secondary to his destructive power. He is a god who dominates, and he creates beings who are made to be dominated.

Genesis likewise presents a correspondence between human and divine nature. This mirroring is made explicit in the *imago Dei* language of chapter one. But the God of Genesis is not violent. His creative work, even when separating one thing from another, is a *bringing together* rather than a *splitting apart*. He is a God who loves, and he creates beings who are made to love and be loved. This is our *telos*, our ultimate end: communion with God and with one another.

The Genesis narrative follows an entropic trajectory from harmony to fragmentation: the original wholeness of Eden disintegrates, layer by layer, into conflict and division. That's what sin is, ultimately: a corruption of wholeness, an unraveling. Ours is an origin story that ends in exile, Adam and Eve expelled from Eden and left to wander the earth.

Could this be a vision of freedom, perhaps? Man, no longer corralled in God's garden and encumbered by God's rules, liberated to find his own meaning, seek his own destiny? That is what freedom has become for us, in our historical moment. Stripped from teleology, freedom has been reduced to permissiveness, pushing past limits, transgressing boundaries. But in Genesis, the exile from Eden is not triumphant; it is funereal, weighted down by the pall of death.

We are confronted in our time with two divergent understandings of freedom: on the one hand, freedom according to postmodernity, an open-ended process of self-definition whose only limit is death; on the other, freedom as an ever-deepening sense of belonging and wholeness, not only within oneself, but in relation to all that is.

When I consider these two different ways of understanding freedom, two images come to mind. The first is a body wheeling endlessly through space: movement without limits. The second comes from Saint Hildegard of Bingen, a medieval mystic. In one of her fiery visions, she sees all of creation as a cosmic wheel, a series of concentric circles, seamlessly interlocking. The outermost layer is divine fire, signifying the power of God that sustains all things. Each subsequent layer is a mixture of physical elements—fire, water, air—and spiritual forces, the invisible working through the realm of the visible. In the center of the wheel, in cruciform stance, stands a human being, arms outstretched, as if waiting to welcome, to receive. Rays of light cut across the wheel, originating from the layer of divine fire, crisscrossing to form a golden web. These rays are beams of power, channels of divine life and strength that form a harmonizing tension, keeping the wheel in perfect balance. "Thus", writes Hildegard, "one part of creation is restrained by another part of creation, and likewise each is sustained by the other."[2]

According to the divine voice that interprets her visions, "divinity is like a wheel, whole and utterly undivided", a circle that "surrounds and contains all that lies inside of it."[3] The image of the human being within the hub of the wheel "signifies that humankind exists within the structure of the universe."[4] If the wheel is a symbol for the integral unity of all of creation, the body-soul unity of the human being is a microcosm, an icon in miniature, of the cosmos as a whole. "The human being", writes Hildegard, "contains the likeness of heaven and earth within her."[5]

The contemporary wisdom of the Church affirms Hildegard's medieval wisdom. The human being must be understood in relation to the cosmos. Pope Francis expounds on this foundational idea in his encyclical

---

[2] Hildegard of Bingen, *The Book of Divine Works*, trans. Nathaniel M. Campbell (Washington, D.C.: Catholic University of America Press, 2018), 84.

[3] Hildegard, *Divine Works*, 54.

[4] Hildegard, *Divine Works*, 62.

[5] Hildegard of Bingen, *Selected Writings* (London: Penguin Books, 2005), 209.

Laudato si', which calls attention to the need to care for the environment. When we hear the words "nature" and "environment", we reflexively think of nonhuman life, plants and animals, as well as nonliving matter, like mountains and rivers. Francis draws the human person into the ecological sphere, not as an observer or controller but as an organism.

This holistic approach recognizes and proclaims the interdependence of all life. We cannot afford to consider human flourishing apart from the environment, like some technocrats are prone to do. Neither can we make the error of those environmentalists who see humankind as a blight on the earth. Both of these polarized perspectives locate human beings as something separate from nature. Avoiding both extremes, we must pursue an *integral ecology*, says Francis: an ecology that takes a view of the whole, perceiving the necessary integration of its many parts. The spiritual, biological, political, moral, technological—all these dimensions of existence must be considered together.

One can trace this holistic thread through all the recent popes. In 2011, Benedict XVI prefigured Francis by emphasizing the importance of ecology, the imperative to "listen to the language of nature" and "answer accordingly". This includes, he says, an attention to the "ecology of man", to our own nature, which must be respected rather than manipulated. Personal wholeness requires listening to one's nature and accepting oneself, acknowledging that we are not self-created. "In this way, and in no other", Benedict writes, "is true human freedom fulfilled."[6] This statement succinctly expresses the connection between identity, teleology, and freedom. It

---

[6] Benedict XVI, Apostolic Address (Berlin, September 22, 2011).

is in recognizing God as Creator that we find our identity; this recognition reveals our purpose, and the fulfillment of our purpose makes us free.

John Paul II's letter *Orientale lumen* connects this discussion directly to the liturgy, which unites bodily and cosmic reality in a shared cry of thanksgiving. Through sacramental worship, "the whole universe is called to recapitulation in Christ." In the Eucharist, we are brought out of fragmenting dualism, and "the body becomes a place made luminous by grace and thus fully human." The liturgy of the Church reveals "the Eucharistic potential of the created world", opening the possibility of restoring exterior harmony with the cosmos, as well as interior harmony within oneself.[7]

I share all these passages to demonstrate that the Church has always proclaimed this manifold truth—from Scripture, to Hildegard, to all the popes of my lifetime. To be Christian is to regard oneself in relation to the cosmos and the cosmos in relation to God. Moreover, how we choose to relate to one of these—self, creation, God—subtly influences how we relate to all of them. I cannot truly honor creation if I do not honor my own body, which is itself a part of creation. Francis emphasizes this connection in a passage from *Laudato si'* that is worth quoting in its entirety:

> The acceptance of our bodies as God's gift is vital for welcoming and accepting the entire world as a gift from the Father and our common home, whereas thinking that we enjoy absolute power over our own bodies turns, often subtly, into thinking that we enjoy absolute power over creation. Learning to accept our body, to care for it

[7] John Paul II, apostolic letter *Orientale lumen* (The Light of the East) (May 2, 1995), no. 11.

and to respect its fullest meaning, is an essential element of any genuine human ecology. Also, valuing one's own body in its femininity or masculinity is necessary if I am going to be able to recognize myself in an encounter with someone who is different. In this way we can joyfully accept the specific gifts of another man or woman, the work of God the Creator, and find mutual enrichment. It is not a healthy attitude which would seek "to cancel out sexual difference because it no longer knows how to confront it."[8]

That final sentence takes a jab at the gender paradigm, referencing a catechesis from 2015 in which Francis critiques gender theory explicitly. He rightly sees that a disembodied concept of gender is something that ultimately erases sexual difference. Our ability to embrace the beauty of the world is connected to our ability to embrace the givenness of our own bodies.

The body is a gift. That is the Christian view. Embodiment binds us to all other life, all other matter. Think of the intimacy of taking a breath—drawing the exhalation of other organisms into your lungs, borrowing a bit of their life to sustain yours. Think of the intimacy of eating—welcoming the matter of plants and animals, absorbing it into your flesh, drawing strength and energy from the fruit of the earth. Think of the intimacy of walking, trusting in each moment that the ground will hold you up, a trust so implicit it remains unthought. It is not the *idealized* body that is a gift—the body adorned with ornamental muscle, the body with long limbs and smooth skin, the airbrushed body suspended in the amber of perpetual health and conventional beauty. We find the body's giftedness within its finitude, its limits and flaws, because these limits reveal to

---

[8] Francis, encyclical letter *Laudato si'* (May 24, 2015), no. 155.

us our interdependence and awaken us to our ultimate vocation: to give and receive love.

Our bodies are not aesthetic objects; they are modes of belonging. Our bodies are continual reminders to us that we are not autonomous, that the fantasy of self-creation is no more than a fever dream, a symptom of underlying illness. "There is, in practice, no such thing as autonomy," writes Wendell Berry, "there is only a distinction between responsible and irresponsible dependence."[9]

Berry isn't Catholic, but I forget that when I'm reading him. He's hard to categorize without stacking up the hyphens: a farmer-philosopher-poet-gadfly. This is because his thought stretches to regard the whole, refusing to be siloed into one academic niche or another, into splintered and myopic specializations. According to Berry, the underlying malady of our culture *is* the inclination toward fragmentation. We disrupt the unity of creation by splitting spirit from body, culture from nature, sexuality from fertility. "It is not possible to devalue the body and value the soul", he writes, and I want to adapt that statement, swapping "soul" for "self".[10] *It is not possible to embrace oneself by rejecting one's body.*

Moreover, Berry describes how "contempt for the body" leads to "contempt for other bodies: the bodies of slaves, laborers, women, animals, plants, the earth itself."[11] I can't help but add to his list: the bodies of the infirm, the unborn, the aged, the disabled, the desolate. This book has been largely concerned with the erasure of sexed embodiment and the triumph of disincarnate gender, but that is only one symptom of a broader disease: divesting the

[9] Wendell Berry, *The Art of the Commonplace* (Berkeley, CA: Counterpoint Press, 2003), 107.

[10] Berry, *Art of the Commonplace*, 101.

[11] Berry, *Art of the Commonplace*, 101.

human body of intrinsic dignity and worth—forgetting the body as *gift*.

Symbol

The cure for this disease cannot be its cause. The balm for dis-integration cannot be found in further entropy. Many of the self-told stories from within the gender paradigm express a desire to feel at home with oneself and at home in the world. That's what I hear behind these stories: the clamor of genuine human longing. This desire for wholeness needs to be named and recognized as *good*. Here's the tragic irony: the people caught up in the gender paradigm are pursuing wholeness within a framework of fragmentation.

Let's retrace our steps a bit. In the slow turn from the medieval to the modern era, the cosmic wheel envisioned by Hildegard is dismantled, piece by piece. The sacramental cosmos becomes a mechanistic universe. The Living Light that speaks to Hildegard through dazzling images becomes a distant clock-winder. Matter no longer sings the things of God, but merely echoes back the hollow sound of human voices. The dome of the heavens flattens into a blank, white sky.

Modernity cracks apart the macrocosm, and the solitary self is hatched, a self no longer open and porous to transcendence, but buffered and insular, convinced of its self-sufficiency. Under this new banner of autonomy, female embodiment becomes a threat. Women's bodies are too porous, too open to the selfhood of another. Pregnancy and maternity belie the modern ideal of the autonomous self. Thus female fertility is pathologized and suppressed, treated as a disease. Sexuality and fertility become disconnected, and the life-giving potential of sex recedes from consciousness. Biological sex is no longer understood in terms of procreative potential, and without a sense of this unifying function, sex is seen as a disparate cluster of characteristics that have no intrinsic cohesion. By now we are entering postmodernity; the dismantling of the microcosm—the human being herself—has begun.

The postmodern self is more vulnerable to external forces: not to transcendence, but to power. In the origin myth of postmodernity, the creator god is Society. Postmodernity inverts the hylomorphic view of the human person; we are not bodies animated by interior souls, but bodies shaped by external forces. *Gender* emerges as a way of naming the cultural production of "man" and "woman". Initially, gender is still linked to the body, as a kind of cultural couture, the pageantry by which a particular society articulates sexual difference. Within a few decades, the ground shifts. Sexual difference *itself* is seen as a costume, a performance that gives the illusion of an essence. Gender is now detached from sex—woman from female, man from male—and grounded in cultural stereotypes. Unmoored from bodily sex, the categories of gender endlessly replicate; each "style" of gender that departs from a strict norm must be encoded and named, given its place in the drop-down menu. The living person at the center of the cosmic wheel, the human being whose body-soul unity mirrors the harmony of the whole—this has been displaced by a fragmentary model of identity. The self is no longer a microcosm, but a smashed idol.

In our postmodern moment, discussions about gender tend to revolve around appearance and roles. To be a woman is to fulfill a particular social role, or to mimic typical feminine behavior and attire. Feminism and its progeny, gender theory, centers the conversation on *doing* rather than *being*. Even in its earlier, loosely religious iterations, feminism had weak metaphysics; the focus was on securing legal rights for women and then, later, on disrupting rigid sex roles. Gender theory developed in a philosophical context that explicitly denies metaphysics, placing the emphasis on "doing gender" (and undoing gender, and redoing gender). In this paradigm, even raising the question of *being* is a mortal sin. Because of this aversion, neither feminism nor gender theory successfully uphold the notion of a woman's intrinsic value and identity, irrespective of action or role. Only the Catholic Christian paradigm provides this. To see it, one must venture under the canopy of a sacramental cosmos and begin to think about sex entirely differently: in terms not of role or performance, but of *symbol*.

We inherit the word *symbol* from the Greeks, and in its literal sense, *symbolon* means to throw or bring together. Its antonym is *diabolon*, which means to split apart. Consider these roots in the context of the Genesis cosmology. God's action in the world is fundamentally an action of creating order out of the chaotic void. When he makes distinctions, separating one form from another, he does so for the purpose of creating balance out of difference. Even the creation of woman follows this pattern. He takes part of the man's body and makes a new life form, a woman who is both like and unlike him. There is a necessary separation between them. But as soon as God creates woman, he brings the man and the woman together; their difference makes possible a communion of love between them. The cosmos is characterized, above all, by harmony.

Now consider the serpent. His words and actions disrupt this original harmony. Evil, in this cosmology, is presented as a force that *divides*. What was created to be in balance is now in conflict. Soul and body, man and woman, people and the earth, the human and the divine—every layer of the cosmic totality is now riven with division. That is what *el diablo* does. The *diabolic* is ultimately a force of fragmentation, discord. It splits apart and disrupts meaning. The *symbolic* is a force that brings together, creating equilibrium in order to reveal meaning. Genesis and gender theory are two incommensurable frameworks, two distinct ways of understanding human personhood. One draws together; the other splits apart.

The gender paradigm is diabolic, in the literal sense. I realize this is a provocative statement, but I also believe that it is true. It is a framework that deceives people, whispers the enthralling lie that we can be our own gods, our own makers, that the body has no intrinsic meaning or dignity, that we can escape our facticity and find refuge in a tailor-made self. In this framework, sex, a reality that encompasses the whole person, is fragmented into disparate features. Woman is cut off from femaleness, a disembodied category that anyone can appropriate. This paradigm takes the human desire for conversion, rebirth, resurrection and bends that desire toward a cheap counterfeit. Interior agony and emptiness are projected onto a healthy body, which then becomes an easy scapegoat, a concrete "problem" that can be "solved". The problem is not the body. The problem is the very real and painful experience of disintegration, a problem that can have any variety of sources, depending on each person's circumstances. This problem of disintegration can't be solved by a philosophy that is ultimately nihilistic, that denies the possibility of meaning beyond the self, and in this way denies the possibility of wholeness.

The Genesis paradigm is symbolic, in the fullest sense. The term *symbol* gives us two layers of signification to work with: first, the sense of drawing together; second, the sense of representation. A symbol draws together seemingly disparate things in order to reveal truth, to disclose multilayered meaning that includes the concrete while simultaneously going beyond it. In the Catholic sacramental imagination, the temporal reveals the eternal. The visible world discloses the invisible. Beyond mere empiric or concrete functions, the stuff of the world holds a symbolic purpose. Our sensible reality makes tangible to us the things of God.

The human body, as part of the material world—indeed, its most noble aspect, alone capable of recognizing divine disclosures—serves as sacred symbol, particularly in its dual incarnation. There is no unsexed human being, and the continuation of our existence depends upon maleness and femaleness. Contrary to the innovations of gender theory, which speak of sex as something not read from the body but arbitrarily imputed to it, the Catholic view holds that there is a *givenness* to our bodies; they are inscribed with sacred meaning that is not determined or constructed by our whim. Bodies speak the language of symbol, with or without our permission.

What, then, is this symbolic meaning? What divine truth do we proclaim through our sexed bodies? Sacred Scripture and tradition give us a central metaphor to understand the relationship between God and humankind: this is the metaphor of conjugal union. This is an intensely bodily metaphor, evoking the image of man and woman becoming one flesh. Such union is made possible by complementary sexual difference. To speak in crudely biological terms: in sexual union, the couple joins their incomplete reproductive systems to become a complete reproductive unit. Both man and woman bring to this coupling the intrinsic potential to create a new person; they have within themselves the seeds of life. But the modes of their potentialities are not identical. The man has the capacity to transmit life outside of himself, while the woman has the potential to gestate new life within.

If we take these biological realities as a mirror for God and humankind, the male sex is analogous to God because God endows life from himself but stands apart from it; he transcends. The female sex is representative of humankind because its power lies in *receptivity*; the human being is created to receive the love of God, be inwardly transformed, and let that love bear fruit.

Receptivity to God, embodied in the form of woman, is humanity's ultimate purpose. This is the *telos* of our existence: to say yes to divine grace, to be subsumed by divine love, and to welcome the inner metamorphosis it brings. Woman, then, is the representative human being before God; she carries the image of this receptivity to which all are beckoned, male and female alike.

We are unused to thinking about sex in symbolic terms, so it is easy to misunderstand the argument. I am not here suggesting that all women must be mothers in the literal sense or that women are more spiritual than men or that men are more proximate to God. These objections forget that we are dealing with *a metaphor of the relation*, not of God or humanity in isolation. Each sex is telling the same story of divine-human communion through the language of the body, albeit from two distinct angles. To put it another way, paraphrasing the words of Pope Francis, the beauty of God's creative design inscribes the image of God not on man and woman in isolation from one another, but in their alliance.[12]

Men do not have some shared capacity, skill, or accomplishment that women do not, and vice versa—no, their

---

[12] Francis, General Audience (April 15, 2015).

bodies simply point toward different spiritual realities. In the same way that water naturally symbolizes that which cleanses and quenches, the male form evokes the image of husband and father, as the female form does mother and bride. This symbolic taxonomy imbues each body with divine significance, especially those our culture deems most worthless, like the ailing, the aging, the dying: "It is the lonely woman upon her sickbed who can but carry the growing Christ within her own soul."[13]

The sacramental, analogical imagination of Catholicism shifts the value of sexed identity from an extrinsic act to intrinsic dignity: from *doing* to *being*. This opens the possibilities of sex-lived-out, freeing us from constricting stereotypes and compelled performance.[14] Bodily sex is not made purposeful through mandated tasks, restrictive temporal roles, or fashionable aesthetics. The supreme meaning of the sexed body is to be a living, visible icon, one who gestures continually toward the world beyond the veil.

†

There is much in life we can't control, such as when we are born and where—the family, country, and history we inherit as time-and-place-bound beings. We enter the story of the world *in medias res*. We don't choose our sex or the path of development it takes. We don't choose our unique amalgam of qualities and traits, those threads that form the tapestry of personality. We cannot choose when illness and trauma will strike; we can only know that they will.

---

[13] Gertrud von le Fort, *The Eternal Woman* (San Francisco: Ignatius Press, 2010), 104.

[14] I acquired the phrase "sex-lived-out" from Angela Franks, as an alternate term for gender that keeps it connected to the body.

Yet there is one thing we can freely choose—*free* only because the gentle fingers of God have loosed what binds and blinds us. We can choose to receive all these things as *gift*. We can choose to say yes to a Love that is stronger than death. We can enter, even now, the eternal moment of Annunciation, when the *yes* of one woman becomes the fulcrum of redemption.

She is the true microcosm, the pinnacle of created being, the living symbol of power-as-surrender. Her *yes* is the power of the creature, a power that opens the severed branch to the greening vigor of God—dead no longer, but erupting in blooms. Her *yes* is the door into Eden, the gate into wholeness, where man is reconciled with woman and both are reconciled with God. In this *yes* is our purpose. In this *yes* is true freedom. Through this *yes*, our vision can be restored; we can see and enter the scope of the whole, the web of fire that holds us in being and tethers us to all other life. Through this *yes*, we become who we are.

O Lord, open thou my lips.

INDEX